The Family Book

AMAZING
THINGS TO DO TOGETHER

Text supplied by Complete Editions
Illustrated by David Woodroffe
Edited by Philippa Wingate
Designed by seagulls.net

Disclaimer: The publisher and authors disclaim as far as is legally permissible
all liability for accidents or injuries or loss that may occur as a result of
information or instructions given in this book.

Advice: Always make sure that children are closely supervised by a responsible
person when engaged in any of the practical activities mentioned in this book,
particularly if they are using matches or scissors. Stay within the law and local rules,
and be considerate of other people.

First published in Great Britain in 2007 by
Michael O'Mara Books Limited, 9 Lion Yard,
Tremadoc Road, London SW4 7NQ

A CIP catalogue record for this book is available from the British Library

ISBN 978-1-906082-10-9

10 9 8 7 6 5 4 3 2 1

www.mombooks.com

Cover design by Angie Allison from an original design by www.blacksheep-uk.com

Printed and bound in Finland by WS Bookwell

Papers used by Michael O'Mara Books are natural, recyclable products made from
wood grown in sustainable forests. The manufacturing processes conform to the
environmental regulations of the country of origin.

The Family Book

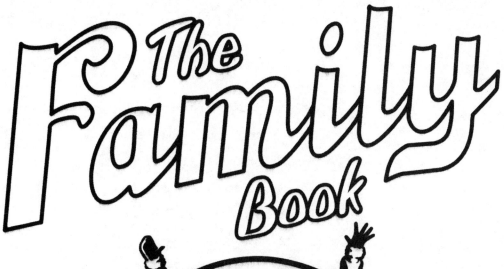

AMAZING
THINGS TO DO TOGETHER

MICHAEL O'MARA BOOK LIMITED

CONTENTS

INTRODUCTION

Hours of fun for all the family are guaranteed. This book is a lucky dip of games to play, tricks to perform, puzzles to solve and life-saving advice. From surviving a volcano to serving the perfect breakfast in bed, there'll never be a dull moment in your household ever again.

However beware, the first in the family to lay hands on this book can use it as a tool of torment and trickery. Make sure you are the one to read about how to set up practical jokes or solve conundrums, and use this against the more gullible members of your clan.

If family feuds loom on the horizon, the answers to any puzzles can be found at the back of the book.

Prepare A Memorable Breakfast In Bed

The key word here is 'prepare' breakfast in bed. This isn't one of those last-minute, 'Please-forgive-me-I'll-never-do-it-again-I-promise', bowl of cereal and mug of instant coffee breakfasts in bed. This one takes some planning and forethought.

You'll need fresh oranges, smoked salmon, free-range eggs, fresh ground coffee, fresh croissants, butter and good quality jam, and a single stem rose (freshly picked). If an adult is the one being treated, add at least a half-bottle of champagne to the list.

Check that the best china is clean, that you have a clean and ironed cloth to fit a breakfast tray, and a clean and ironed napkin. Find a tall, narrow glass vase as well.

BREAKFAST IS SERVED

Lay the tray elegantly with butter on a clean dish (with a butter knife), a cup and saucer, a side plate, fork and two knives, jam with a spoon and sugar with a spoon (if the person takes sugar, and that's something you really should know).

Put the rose in the vase with water and fold the table napkin neatly. Warm two croissants. Squeeze the oranges and pour the juice into a glass jug. Half-fill a champagne glass with orange juice. Chop the smoked salmon into pieces. Make coffee. (If milk is needed, warm some and put it in a jug.) Make scrambled eggs and add the smoked salmon pieces. Spoon this onto a warm plate. Place croissants on the side plate. Fill the champagne flute with chilled champagne, to make Buck's Fizz.

Carry the breakfast to the person you've prepared it for. Remember to knock on the bedroom door before entering. You never know, if you're lucky, you might be left a piece of croissant and a sip of Buck's Fizz when it's time to clear the dishes.

CONVINCE YOUR NEIGHBOURS YOU HAVE WON THE LOTTERY

Some people who win the lottery appear in newspapers and on television and everyone knows they have suddenly become millionaires. But there are others who keep their good luck to themselves and the only way their neighbours discover what has happened to them is by picking up on little clues. People will be convinced you have won the lottery if you use clues and hints like these.

* When there is a big lottery win close to where you live, refuse to gossip about it.

* Arrange for luxury cars to arrive at your house for demonstration drives.

* Order catalogues from very expensive shops and leave these around the house for people to see when they visit – the same goes for very expensive holiday brochures.

* Get members of the family to ring home when people are with you. Answer the call, but keep your voice to a whisper. Pretend that the conversation you are having is about a huge sum of money or a very expensive home security system.

* Start talking about a very expensive restaurant, or a treat for the family you couldn't normally afford, or the idea of giving up work for good – and then stop yourself suddenly, saying something like: 'Oh – I shouldn't have said that. You won't mention it to anyone else, will you?'

* Buy pieces of expensive-looking fake jewellery for Mum to wear. Make sure she pretends to try and cover them up so other people can't see them. Dad could get a really expensive-looking watch, but keep pulling his sleeve down to cover it up.

* When you're talking to neighbours repeat phrases like: 'Money doesn't matter. It's friends that really count.'

How To Go Tobogganing If You Don't Have A Toboggan

Has the snow ever caught you out? You think the winter is over. You decide to wait until next winter before getting a toboggan. Then you wake up one morning to find everything is covered in white and every toboggan for miles around has been snapped up by other families in the same situation.

Don't despair. You can still have a great time in the snow by making snow-sliding toys of your own.

TRAYS, SACKS AND SKATEBOARDS

Toboggans work because they slide over snow. So if you can find other things at home that do the same, make do with these and enjoy the snow while it lasts.

✳ Kitchen trays made of plastic, or better still metal, make great snow sliders. You'll be closer to the ground than on a toboggan (much closer), but you can either sit on the tray and steer with your hands, or lie down head-first and steer with your feet.

✳ Plastic sacks will put you even closer to the ground – right on it in fact – and if you lie down on one, you can slide over the snow once it is well beaten down.

✳ Using a skateboard will take longer to prepare than a tray or plastic sack, but it will give a firmer ride over the snow. You'll need to unscrew the wheels, so that the bottom of the skateboard is smooth and can slide over the snow. Then you can either sit on the board or lie on it head-first as you whiz down the slope.

✳ If you have surfboards that you use in the sea on summer holidays, you could try these on the snow. Be careful if the boards are made of compressed foam. This could easily snap if the board strikes an obstacle. You will need to turn the board over so the fin is not digging into the snow.

Climb Through A Sheet Of Writing Paper

It may seem unlikely, but it really is possible to make a hole in a sheet of writing paper and climb though it. It takes some working out, though – as you'll soon discover.

Give everyone in your family the same sized sheet of paper. Tell them they can use whatever they like, so long as they end up with a hole big enough for their whole body to get through. (Have spare sheets of paper to replace failed attempts.)

CRUCIAL CUTS

You can actually make this work with a piece of paper as small as 10 x 15cm, providing you use a pair of scissors to cut the paper in a special way. Here's the secret:

1 Fold the sheet of paper in half down the middle.

2 Now make a series of straight cuts in the paper as shown below. Notice that these cuts are made from alternate sides and that they do not go all the way across.

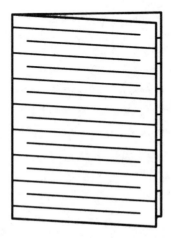

3 Open the sheet of paper and cut along the fold you originally made. But be sure to leave the last strip at either end uncut as shown. This means that you cut along the fold from X to X.

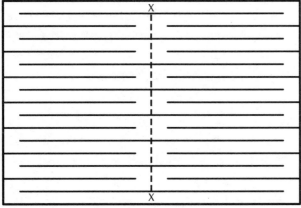

4 Open up the paper carefully and you'll find that you have made a ring large enough to pass over the top of your head, and all the way down your body to your toes. When you look at it another way, you've made a circle out of a lot of straight lines!

Whichever way you see it, you've found a way of climbing through a sheet of writing paper.

MAKE A PHOTOGRAPHIC FAMILY TREE

Finding out about your family helps bring history alive. The best way to keep track of where your relatives and ancestors fit in to your family history is to make a family tree.

The easiest way to do this is to work backwards in time, beginning with yourself. If you've ever seen a family tree, you'll know what one looks like: rows of names, joined by lines, with the most recent names at the bottom and the oldest at the top. That's what your family tree will look like as well, but with photos of as many of the people listed as you can find.

DRAWING THE TREE

1 On family trees, the members of each generation appear on the same line. So, when you begin with the children in your family, write their names at the bottom of a large sheet of paper.

2 Draw a short vertical line above each name and connect these with a horizontal line. That's the youngest generation taken care of on the family tree.

3 Now draw a vertical line upwards from the middle of the one joining the kids.

4 Make a T-shape at the top of this vertical line. Write Dad's name on the left of the line and Mum's name on the right.

5 Write the names of Dad's brothers and sisters to the left of his name, and Mum's brothers and sisters to the right of her name.

6 Join the brothers and sisters in each of these two families with horizontal lines above the two groups of names. Then draw vertical lines to move up a generation to their parents.

7 Repeat the process with the names of the grandparents and their brothers and sisters.

8 Then move up to their parents (the great-grandparents of the kids at the bottom of the family tree).

9 Find a photo of everyone listed on your family tree and stick it beside their name. No one will thank you for ruining the only existing picture of Great Aunt Gertie, so make copies or scans of old pictures so that you can use printouts instead of originals.

10 Continue adding the names of earlier generations as you discover more about your family history.

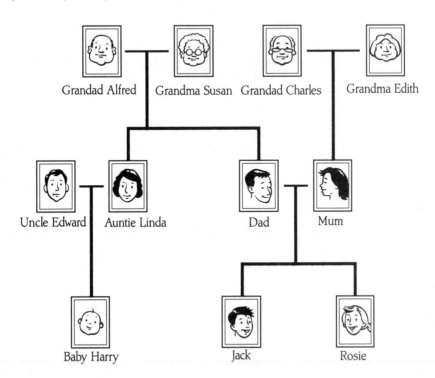

CALCULATE THE HIDDEN SIDES OF TWO DICE

Get someone in the family to stack two dice one on top of the other in any combination they like. Now bet them that you can work out the total number of spots on the three sides hidden from view. It sounds like you need to be a genius, or have some kind of second sight. But the answer is ridiculously simple.

KEY INFORMATION

To work this trick every time, all you need to know is that the number of spots on any two opposite sides of a single dice always adds up to *seven*.

From this it follows that if you subtract the number of spots on the top of the top dice from fourteen (two times seven) you will be left with the total number of spots on the remaining three sides that can't be seen.

So make sure you are the first and only person to read this page. One way of avoiding suspicion is to take your time over giving the answer and appear to be using some form of mind-reading.

PROVE YOU'RE A MATHEMATICAL GENIUS

Here's a way to establish yourself as the household's maths genius. Try out this trick – and prove your prowess by getting everyone else to do all the work for you!

WHAT YOU DO

1 Announce at the start that whatever numbers people choose to use in the calculation you are going to give them, the answer will be 1089 – you know that for a fact. Amazing!

2 Ask someone in the family to write down a number with three digits, in which the first and last digits have a difference of at least *two*.

3 Next get them to write the digits in the reverse order.

4 Ask them to subtract the smaller number from the larger one.

5 Now ask them to write the digits from this answer in reverse order.

6 Get them to add these two numbers together.

7 The answer will be 1089 – as you told them it would be.

HOW IT WORKS

✳ Think of a number	489
✳ Reverse the digits	984
✳ Subtract the smaller number from the higher	984
	− 489
	495
✳ Reverse these digits	594
✳ Add these numbers	+ 495
	= 1089

There you are! You're a genius!

PLAY KIM'S GAME

As a family game that tests everyone's powers of observation and memory, Kim's Game is hard to beat. Dad may think he has X-ray vision. Other people in the family may think they have a keen eye for detail. But this game will prove who has the sharpest eyes and clearest memory in the family.

In *Kim*, the great novel by Rudyard Kipling about nineteenth-century spies in India, the hero (Kim) first acquires his skill as a secret agent by playing this game. If members of your family fancy themselves as future secret agents this game is an ideal way to start their training.

NOW YOU SEE IT . . . NOW YOU DON'T

✳ While the other members of the family are in another room you collect between 20 and 30 objects – as varied as possible – place these on a tray or table and cover them with a cloth.

✳ The rest of the family then gather round the collection.

✳ You remove the cloth and let them study the things you have laid out for 30 seconds.

✳ Then you replace the cloth, hiding all the objects.

✳ Everyone is given a piece of paper and something to write with and then has to list as many of the objects as they can remember.

✳ One point is scored for every object remembered, but a point is deducted for anything listed that isn't actually there.

✳ The player who scores the most points wins.

BALLOON STOMP

This is best played out of doors, in an area where you won't disturb other people, because you are going to make quite a bit of noise! It's not a game to play if Mum and Dad are feeling a bit fragile after a party or a night out. (If you have a dog, make sure it is somewhere where it won't be frightened by loud bangs.)

BANG POP

1. To play Balloon Stomp as a family, it's more fun to give each player two balloons: one for each leg. If there are quite of lot of people playing, they only need one balloon each.

2. Players inflate their balloons and tie them to their ankles with a length of string, so that there is about 30cm between their feet and the balloons.

3. Players spread out before play begins.

4. On the word 'Go' they all try to stomp on other players' balloons and pop them, while protecting their own balloons from being burst.

The last player to have an unpopped balloon wins the game.

SPELLING BEE

This is a quick game for everyone in the family to enjoy. The players sit in a circle and take it in turns to spell a word given to them by the previous player. The words need to be pitched at the right level for each player - don't let Dad get away with giving the difficult ones to everyone else - so choose words that players have a reasonable chance of spelling correctly. (Pass a dictionary round the circle, from player to player, after each turn.)

A player who spells a word correctly scores one point. But if a word is spelt incorrectly, a point is deducted from his or her score. You can play the game for an agreed number of rounds (usually about five minutes). The player with the highest score at the end is the winner.

SUGGESTED WORDS

Acrobat	Cartwheel	Kingdom	Safety
Ancestor	Cylinder	Knuckle	Seed
Barbecue	Degree	Lens	Temper
Billion	Disrespectful	Llama	Together
	Embarrass	Mercury	Ubiquitous
	Entwine	Mosquito	Unless
	Feeble	Netball	Vanilla
	Firework	Nowhere	Volcano
	Gangway	Obstinate	Wallpaper
	Granddaughter	Oversleep	Watch
	Handkerchief	Palace	Xylophone
	Hermit	Phantom	Yawn
	Include	Quack	Yesterday
	Igloo	Quicksand	Young
	Jungle	Rail	Zigzag
	Jury	Result	Zoological

TRYING TRIANGLES

Position the book so that everyone in the family can see this page. Then ask them to study this diagram and say how many triangles can be found in it. There are probably more than you may imagine. You'll find the answer on page 187.

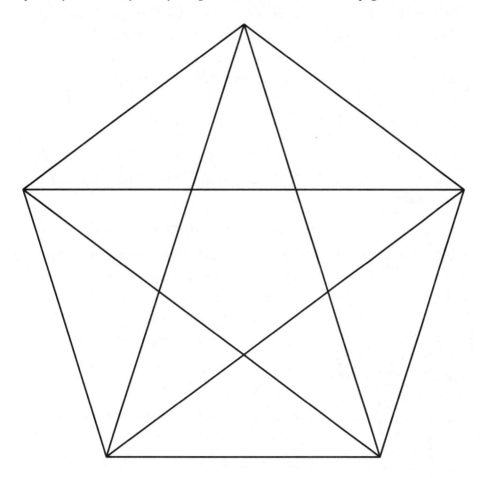

SAVING THE PLANET

Saving planet earth may look like an enormous task and the 'green' things people do at home may seem very small when measured against it – *but* if every family did just some of the things listed here, they would all make a huge difference to saving the earth from the terrible damage caused by pollution, greenhouse gases, global warming, growing deserts, rainforest destruction and rising sea levels.

Work out a system of rewards for the greenest member of your family, and decide on suitable punishments for the household's eco-criminals.

SAVING ENERGY AT HOME

✳ If someone complains it's cold, don't turn up the heating, fetch them a jumper.

✳ Buy energy-saving light bulbs and replace the old ones.

✳ Switch off lights when they aren't needed.

✳ Turn off electrical equipment when it isn't being used, for example: games consoles, TV sets, DVD players and recorders, hi-fi systems and radios. Check that the red stand-by lights are off; if they are still shining, the appliances are still using electricity.

✳ Run washing machines at lower temperatures using low-temperature detergents.

✳ Keep doors and windows closed and block any draughts with draught excluders.

✳ Put extra insulation in the roof and around the hot-water tank.

✳ Walk or cycle short distances. Travel longer distances by train. Try to use the car less.

SAVE WATER

✳ Don't run taps when you wash your hands or face. Put the plug in the basin and fill with a sensible amount of water.

✳ Don't run the cold tap when you brush your teeth. Fill a glass with water to rinse your teeth.

✳ Take short showers instead of baths.

✳ Share bath water – if you dare.

✳ Fit a water-saving device in the WC cistern.

✳ Make sure everyone in the family remembers this lovely rhyme which is all about reducing the number of times you flush the loo:

> *If it's yellow, let it mellow.*
> *If it's brown flush it down.*

✳ Don't run taps to rinse plates – use a bowl of clean water instead.

✳ Install a water butt in the garden to collect rainwater, which you can use to water plants.

✳ Use bath water to water plants. It's only wasted down the drain.

How To Tell If Dad Has Been Replaced By An Alien

Guessing that Dad is no longer Dad can be tricky because many aliens have far more advanced brains than humans. This means that they can control what you are thinking. So the whole family can be conned into thinking that they're talking to Dad, when really it's an alien who looks like Dad.

DANGER SIGNS

✳ A large spacecraft parked outside the house is a useful indication of alien visitors. The family ought to be a little suspicious.

✳ Even if there isn't a visible spacecraft, aliens and their craft have a disastrous effect on electrical appliances. So if the TV explodes, the radio keeps leaping from one channel to another, the computer plays all Mum's favourite songs at full volume non-stop and the washing-machine goes on spinning until it blows up – the family would be right to think that something strange is happening.

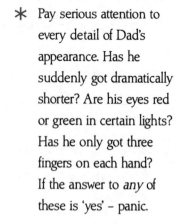

✳ Pay serious attention to every detail of Dad's appearance. Has he suddenly got dramatically shorter? Are his eyes red or green in certain lights? Has he only got three fingers on each hand? If the answer to *any* of these is 'yes' – panic.

✱ With their advanced brains, aliens can do things humans can't do. Test the potential alien to see if he can do things faster than Dad would usually. Try asking him to programme the TV recorder. If the 'Dad' being tested gets that right first time, something odd is going on.

✱ Alternatively, give 'Dad' a Sudoku puzzle. If he fills in the numbers as quickly as he fills in his weekly lottery card, there's definitely a different brain at work in his head.

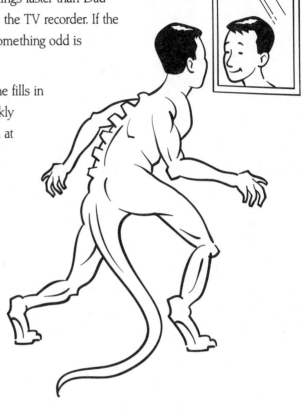

ALIEN CHALLENGE

Although aliens seem to be superior to humans in lots of ways, there are some simple things in the human world that they can't deal with.

✱ Aliens are often confused by stairs. If the family all run upstairs and Dad has difficulty following, it may not be because he has eaten too much.

✱ Mirrors confuse aliens as well. Try holding a mirror in front of 'Dad' and see how he reacts. When he keeps patting the glass, to touch his reflection, that has to be a big giveaway. When was the last time Dad showed any interest in a mirror?

✱ What about water? A lot of aliens can't stand it. If the family squirt water at alien Dad and he runs away in terror, this is further proof.

✱ Another feature of human life that sends aliens into a panic is the common cold. Aliens have no resistance to the bugs and germs that humans have to deal with. Start sneezing and coughing in front of the alien that has replaced Dad and check out the reaction.

Dicey Mind-Reading

Just in case you need to remind other people that you have super-human mind-reading powers, try this extraordinary feat of mental agility.

All you need is:

* Three dice

* One unsuspecting subject

* One brain (capable of doing simple mental arithmetic)

WHAT YOU DO

1 Ask a member of the family to roll three dice, so that you cannot see them.

2 Ask them to double the number on the first dice.

3 Ask them to add 3 to that new number.

4 Ask them to multiply the answer by 5.

5 Ask them to add the number on the second dice.

6 Multiply all this by 10.

7 Ask them, finally, to add the number on the third dice.

8 Ask them for the total.

9 All you then do is subtract 150 from this total and you will have a three-digit number.

Now comes the clever bit:

10 The first digit of the three-digit number will be the number shown on the first dice.

11 The second digit will be the number on the second dice.

12 The third number will be the digit on the third dice.

CHECK IT YOURSELF

✳ Imagine the first dice shows   **4**

✳ Double it   8

✳ Add 3   11

✳ Multiply by 5   55

✳ Add second dice (say it shows **6**)   61

✳ Multiply by 10   610

✳ Add third dice (say **2**)   612

✳ Subtract 150   – 150

✳ And ... what do you have?   **462**

Jackpot!

How to Get Rescued in a Desert

The family is champing at the bit to drive across a desert, a thrilling adventure and amazing scenery – but are you prepared? A lot of people who need to be rescued in desert areas only set off to make short trips. They aren't as well prepared for emergencies as for long-range expeditions travelling in the desert for a week or more. So when they run into problems, they seldom have the proper equipment to get themselves out of trouble, or to make contact with people who could rescue them.

GET LOST

It's bad enough if the vehicle you're travelling in breaks down in the desert, but things can get much worse if you get lost as well – this is where the biggest danger lies. When this happens, Dad will probably think he can find his way to safety just following his instincts, but this usually is more likely to have you driving round in circles instead of doing what you should be doing: making it easy for rescuers to find you.

GOLDEN RULES

There are two golden rules for the family to follow:

1. The first is to make sure that someone at your destination knows which route you are taking and when you expect to arrive. If this person realises that you haven't turned up as planned, he or she can alert the rescue services and a search can be started.

2. The second rule of desert travel is to realise early on that you are lost. If you accept that fact right away, you can stop and organise what to do. Unfortunately too many people keep pressing on, using up time, fuel, water and their own energy, hoping that they will somehow reach safety – sadly, very few of them ever do.

WHAT NEXT?

OK – the family has done the right thing and acknowledged that you are lost in the desert. What happens next? Quite simply, go to the closest point where you can easily be spotted from the air. This could be the nearest high ground, or, if there is no high ground nearby, head for the nearest flat, open stretch of desert. In either case, it will be easier for rescuers to see you there than if you are hidden in a gully or wadi.

ATTRACT ATTENTION

The next thing you should do is to make preparations for attracting attention. A search plane flying low can appear very quickly, so you need to have everything ready to catch the pilot's eye at a moment's notice. Being lost in the desert is frightening, so keeping everyone in the family busy will help take your minds off your predicament – and there's plenty of work to do.

The natural world has very few straight lines, so you should try to create a regular pattern of some sort – one that's big enough to be spotted from the air. A vehicle on its own may not be that obvious from the air, but you can make it look much bigger by placing large objects in a regular pattern beside it.

Take the driving mirrors off the car and keep them in a convenient place; a flashing object will attract attention more quickly than almost anything else. If you take the metal backing off a mirror and scratch a fine cross through the coating, you will find that you can 'sight' it on the plane, and by tilting the mirror backwards and forwards you are much more likely to be accurate in catching the pilot's attention.

REGULAR PATTERNS

If you find yourself in an area of scrub, see if you can uproot bushes immediately round your vehicle and place them between the nearest ones still growing, so that you create a dense ring surrounding an open space, in the centre of which is your vehicle. Alternatively move rocks to form a circle around the car.

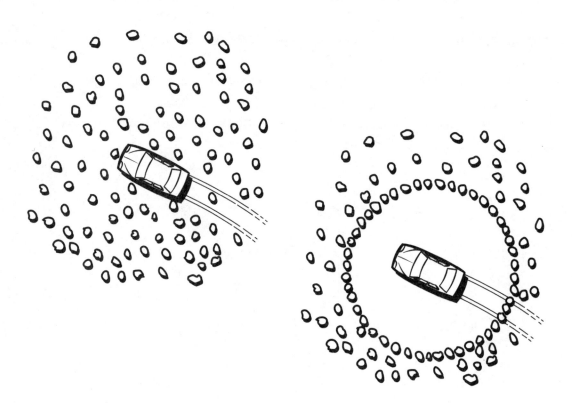

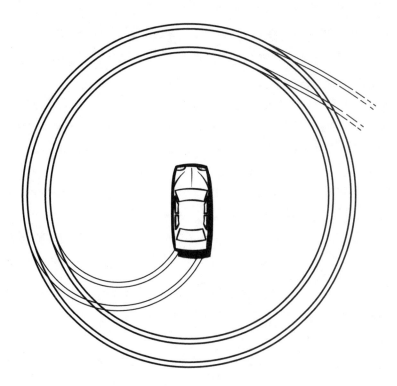

Maybe the desert you are in is very sandy. No problem – all you have to do is drive the vehicle round in a wide circle to form two deep parallel ruts and then park in the centre of it.

You can form other patterns by digging trenches deep enough to throw shadows. You could try making the trenches in the shape of the international rescue message SOS, which can be read from two directions.

Prepare a fire with things from the car that will burn, such as seat covers and floor mats. Set them alight when a rescue plane comes into sight and the smoke will lead rescuers right to where you are.

If you can do all these things, they'll make you feel much more positive about the situation you're in – and they'll make it a whole lot easier for searchers to rescue you than if you don't.

PLAY THE PARSON'S CAT

The Parson's Cat is a great game for the family because people of any age can play. It doesn't require any equipment, because it's a word game. It's ideal to play on car journeys or to fill in time while you're waiting at an airport.

The aim of the game is to describe the parson's cat with adjectives beginning with the first letter of the alphabet (A) and then all the other letters one by one. Every player has a go at using the same letter, before play moves on to the next letter and so on through the alphabet from A to Z.

A simpler version, which might be more suitable for younger players, begins with one player using an adjective with A, the next an adjective beginning with B, the third an adjective beginning with C and so on.

In both versions some letters will be easier than others and X and Y are probably best left out altogether.

FULL VERSION EXAMPLE

✳ The first player announces, 'The parson's cat is an amiable cat.'

✳ The second player follows with, 'The parson's cat is an athletic cat.'

✳ The third player says, 'The parson's cat is an agile cat'

✳ And so it continues until every player has had a go.

✳ Then the first player begins on the Bs with 'The parson's cat is a beautiful cat.'

✳ And the others follow as they work through the alphabet.

BOGGLE YOUR BRAIN WITH 'ABRACADABRA'

ABRACADABRA is, of course, a word used by magicians. In days gone by it was also used as an amulet or charm to ward off disease. The word would be written on a piece of parchment, which was hung round the wearer's neck. An especially effective way of writing the charm is shown below.

However, the challenge here is to study the triangle of letters in this charm and discover how many ways there are in it to spell the word ABRACADABRA, moving letter by letter through the formation. You should start at the letter A at the top of the formation and move from one letter to an adjacent one. You'll find the answer on page 187.

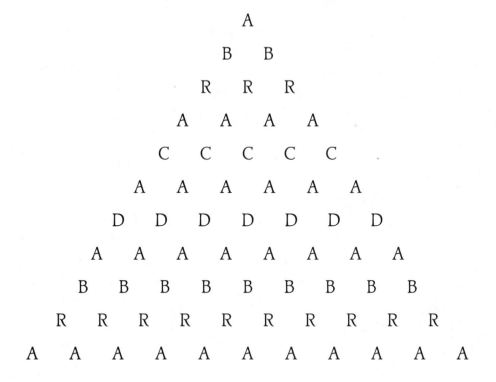

TEST YOUR FAMILY'S TASTE BUDS

Do things taste different when you can't see them? It seems unlikely, but get your family to take this taste test and you'll be surprised by the results.

TASTING TIPS

Choose one person to prepare and organise the test, unobserved. They can use anything in the house for the taste test, but they should try to choose a few ingredients that could taste like more than one thing – raw cauliflower and raw broccoli can be easily confused, for example.

Here's a list of possible taste-test items:

Grape juice, margarine, soft cheese, yoghurt, ham, corned beef, raw carrot, cheddar cheese (give a bonus point for anyone who knows what kind of cheese it is), sardines, raw apple, celery, raw parsnip, cashew nuts, dates, nutmeg, thyme, mint sauce, semolina pudding, seedless grapes, cherries (with their stones removed), and, if you are really mean, shampoo and perfume.

TAKE THE TEST

The rest of the family should sit down round the kitchen table wearing blindfolds. Each person has a sheet of paper and something to write with. The aim of the taste test is for people to decide for themselves and see how accurate their taste buds are. When they have tasted something, they write down what they think it is – without giving clues to other people by saying things like 'Yes – that's sweet. So it could be honey ... or is it syrup?' The writing doesn't have to be neat, because people are blindfolded, so long as everyone can read their answers at the end.

MAKE YOUR FEELINGS KNOWN IN HAND GESTURES

Wouldn't it be great to have some non-verbal ways of letting your family (and other people) know exactly what you are thinking without raising your voice or weeping.

Here are some easy gestures, useful in so many different situations ...

* *Someone is asking for too much pocket money, or the bill for a meal is too much:* Point the first two fingers of either hand at your temple, as though you are going to shoot yourself.

* *You want someone to get lost, particularly if they have just won an argument:* Close your eyes, look down at the ground, raise both hands in front and level with your forehead and shake your hands vigorously as if driving away an unpleasant smell.

* *Someone nearly knocks you off your feet charging down the stairs or a motorist nearly runs you down:* Bend at the waist. Point one hand at your bottom and the other at the offending person.

* *An expression of general disgust – essential on too many occasions to mention:* Adopt a look of outraged displeasure (usually with an open mouth). Hold up both hands, either side of your head and slightly forwards. With your fingers raised shake your hands very slightly and very fast.

* *How to emphasise a complaint:* Adopt the same expression of outraged displeasure (above) but this time, with your elbows held in to your ribs, hold your hands out at waist height and, again, move the hands up and down fast and furiously.

DUMBFOUND THE FAMILY WITH DOODLES

This is a fun way of using a little lateral thinking.

✳ Gather the family so that everyone can see this page, but cover the page until everyone is ready, so that nobody gets a sneak view of these doodles before anyone else.

✳ Make sure that everyone has paper and something to write with.

✳ Explain that they have five minutes to work out what each of the doodles represents.

✳ Tell them not to shout out their answers, but to write them down and keep them well hidden.

✳ When everybody is ready, set the clock and remove the cover so that they can all see . . . The answers are on page 187.

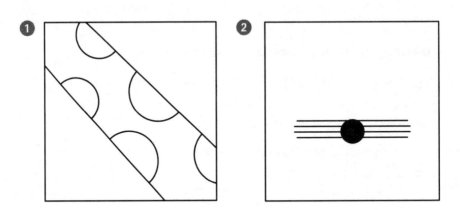

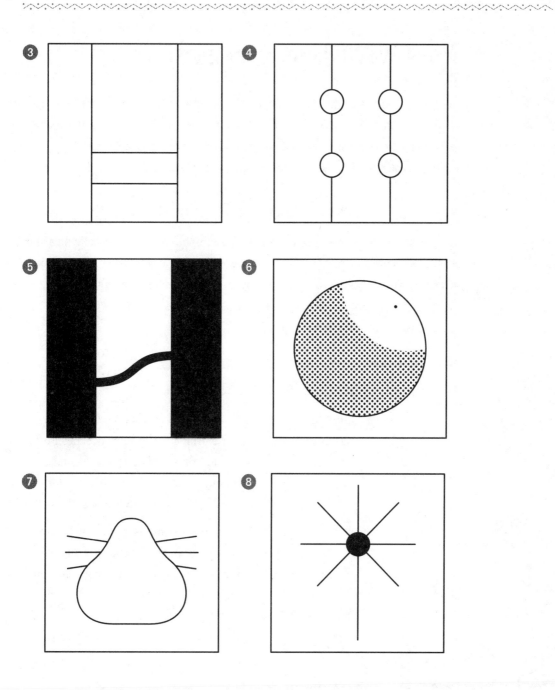

TURN WASTE INTO COMPOST

Garden compost is a crumbly, sweet-smelling fertiliser, which you can easily make at home. It can do wonders for the health and well-being of your plants and your garden in general. Even better, the process of making compost converts waste materials, which would otherwise be thrown away, into something useful.

EQUIPMENT AND CONTENTS

You can make compost in a heap, in a special compost bin, which usually measures about one metre square, or in a wire cage also measuring about one metre square. Whichever you choose, locate the compost in a convenient corner of the garden, where it's out of sight but where you can also get to it easily.

To make compost you will need:

✳ A garden fork

✳ A thick black plastic sheet, or an old piece of carpet

✳ Organic material to turn into compost. This can include: all healthy green garden waste; fruit and vegetable peelings from the kitchen; crushed egg shells; teabags; coffee grounds; annual weeds, such as stinging nettles; grass clippings (but not too many); seaweed (if you are lucky enough to live near the sea).

✳ Compost activator. You can make compost without it, but an activator will speed up the process. Fresh manure is a good natural activator, or you can buy chemical ones at garden centres.

Things best avoided in compost include:

✳ Cooked food

✳ Processed food

✳ Meat, bones and fat

✳ Paper, unless it is finely shredded

✳ Diseased plants and leaves

✳ Perennial weeds such as docks and thistles (unless they are placed in the centre of the compost heap where the heat will destroy their seeds and roots)

WORKING THE MAGIC

The secret of making compost successfully is allowing air to get into the heap and letting it get hot enough. If you build your compost heap correctly, both of these things will happen.

1. Start by spreading a layer of dry, twiggy material at the bottom.

2. Build up the heap in layers 15cm deep.

3. Vary the type of material in each layer and sprinkle each one with manure or activator (if you are using it).

4. Place the black plastic, or old carpet, on top of the heap. Puncture a few holes in the plastic to allow moisture into the compost heap.

5. Put weights on top of the cover to hold it down.

6. Leave the rest to nature. The compost should be ready after three months.

7. If you want to give nature a hand, you can mix up the compost with your garden fork every two to three weeks. Turning compost like this will help speed up the process.

8. When it has matured, dig out the compost and mix it in your garden's soil.

9. Leave aside any material that has not broken down and put this on your next compost heap.

10. If you have two compost heaps, one can be maturing while you are building the second.

CALCULATE WHEN PEOPLE WERE BORN

Presumably you know when the other members of your family were born – imagine the reaction if you forgot someone's birthday!

But what about other people, complete strangers for example? Wouldn't it be something if you were able to work out not only how old they are, but the date they were born and even the day of the week on which they were born? If it sounds too good to be true, read on and discover how you can do just that. (You may find it helpful to have a calculator to hand.)

THE NUMBERS

1 Ask the person to write down (but not tell you) a number showing the day of the week, the date in the month and the month in the year when they were born, in that order. For the days of the week Monday is 1, Tuesday 2, Wednesday 3 etc. For the months January is 1, February 2, March 3 etc.

2 Ask them to double the number they have written down

3 Then add 5

4 Then multiply the number by 50

5 Then add their present age

6 Then subtract 365

7 Then add 115

8 Now ask for the answer

WHAT THE NUMBERS TELL YOU

✳ The day of the week on which your subject was born (shown by the first digit)

✳ The date on which they were born (shown by the second and third digits)

✳ The month in which the subject was born (the next digits)

✳ Your subject's present age (the last digits)

THE WAY IT WORKS

Imagine that your subject was born on Thursday 16 March, 1995, and is now **12** years old. The number written down will be **4** (for Thursday), **16** for the date and **3** (for March) – making **4163**.

✳ So, begin with that number	4163
✳ Multiply by 2	x 2
	8326
✳ Add 5	+ 5
	8331
✳ Multiply by 50	x 50
	416550
✳ Add age (12)	+ 12
	416562
✳ Subtract 365	- 365
	416197
✳ Add 115	+ 115
	416312

There's your magic number **4**, for the day of the week when your subject was born (Thursday), **16** for the date of their birth, **3** for the month in which they were born (March) and finally **12** for their age now.

SNOW ANGELS

When the snow is lying deep and powdery outside, bundle everyone up in warm, waterproof clothing (including hats and gloves) and crunch your way to a place where the snow is still fresh and undisturbed. This will be the perfect place to make snow angels.

1 Line up next to each other, or form a circle.

2 You should be far enough apart that you can't touch the person next to you when you spread out your arms and legs.

3 Let yourself fall gently backwards into the snow.

4 Keep your whole body flat.

5 Move your arms out across the snow from next to your legs until they reach above your head.

6 At the same time move your legs apart as far as you can and then back together again.

7 Continue sweeping them back and forth like this until you have brushed angel patterns into the snow.

8 Ask someone to pull you up, so that you can get to your feet without leaving a handprint or stepping on your snow angel.

HOLIDAY SCAVENGERS

Before you set off on holiday draw up a list of things that every member of the family has to collect. These could be things that you might find only at the place you are visiting, or they could be more general items. The point of the competition is to get everyone in the family collecting. The first one to find everything on the list wins a prize of their choice – as long as it doesn't cost more than an ice cream!

The fun lies in creating your own list, but here are 15 suggestions to set you thinking ...

1. A bus ticket

2. A local newspaper

3. A shop receipt

4. A paper napkin with the name of a café or restaurant

5. A postcard of the national flag, or a real flag

6. A local coin of the lowest value available

7. A small packet of sugar

8. A feather

9. A luggage label

10. A lolly stick

11. A wrapper from a chocolate bar

12. A paper bag with the name of a shop

13. A photograph of the head of state of the country you are in

14. A local postage stamp

15. A flower

Cut A Loop Of Paper In Half And Still Have Only One Piece Of Paper

This is true. It really is possible to cut a loop of paper in half and still end up with just a single piece of paper. Try it on the rest of the family and see how they get on.

GETTING STARTED

To make it fair, give everyone the same things to work with:

* A strip of paper roughly 30cm long by 4cm wide

* A piece of sticky tape to join the ends to form a loop

* A pair of scissors

That's all they need. Tell them to make the paper strip into a loop and then work out how to cut it in half so that there is still only one piece of paper when they have finished.

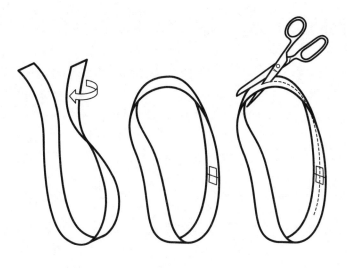

THE TRICK

There's a curious piece of science at work here and, if you understand what it is, you can do precisely what's asked. This is how:

1 Before you stick together the ends of the strip of paper, twist over one end and then stick it to the other.

2 Now use the scissors to cut lengthwise down the centre of the strip.

3 When you have finished, don't expect to end up with two 2cm-wide strips of paper. What you've actually got is another single loop that is twice as long as the original – but only half as wide! Pretty amazing, eh?

What you need to know is that the original loop you made is called a Mobius strip (knowing this is guaranteed to impress all members of the family). A Mobius strip is a real oddity. For instance, it's only got one side, although it appears to have two.

Make another just like you made the first, and prove this to yourself. Take your second strip and draw a pencil line up the centre of it. The whole of the surface of the paper will be marked by the pencil and you'll find that you've made a continuous line without lifting the pencil off the paper.

Solve Roman Number Puzzles

You only need some cocktail sticks to set up and solve these puzzles using Roman numerals. They're quick, fun and easy to do wherever you are. Try them and find out who's the Roman number know-it-all in the family. The answers are on page 187.

1 Make this sum correct by moving one stick.

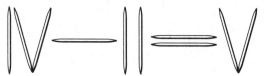

2 Move two sticks to make this sum correct.

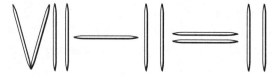

3 Remove three sticks to make this sum correct.

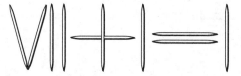

4 Make this sum correct without moving any sticks at all!

SPY CATCHER

Big drama! Your family has come across a spy ring during your holiday by the sea. You've become suspicious of the people who never go to the beach, but spend all their time staring at the harbour through binoculars. They may have bird-watching books with them, but you haven't been fooled. It's not birds they are watching, but ships moving around in the naval base nearby.

Then, one day you discover this strange square of letters left by one of the mysterious 'bird-watchers'. The letters have been written on the page of a newspaper beside the daily crossword. It looks as if someone has been trying to solve a crossword clue and given up, because the newspaper has been left behind on a café table. But you have other ideas.

You don't know what they mean, but you make a quick copy to see if anyone in your family can work out what is going on. It doesn't look as if you have much time, because just after you finished making the copy, the newspaper was collected by someone wearing dark glasses, who studied the page with the square of letters and then made a telephone call.

Set a timer and see who is the first to work out what the letter square means. The answer is on page 187.

S.	H	E	E	O	O
Y					A
N					R
Y			13		T
A					V
S	U	D	C	V	L

BUILD A NEST-BOX

Nest-boxes are easy to build and will attract birds into your garden, where you can enjoy watching them setting up home, fetching food and rearing their young.

TYPES OF NEST-BOX

There are two main types of nest-box. One has a small hole, which attracts birds like tits, pied flycatchers and nuthatches that like to build their nests inside small holes in trees and other secure places. The other type of nest-box has an open front, which attracts birds such as robins, wrens and spotted flycatchers that build nests on ledges.

SIMPLE CONSTRUCTION

Both types of nest-box can be built from a single plank of wood measuring 120cm long, 15cm wide and 2.5cm thick (thick wood keeps birds warm in winter and cool in summer, and also stops the nest-box from twisting out of shape and letting in rain).

To build a nest-box, you will need:

* The plank of wood

* A saw

* A hammer

* A drill

* Galvanised nails (they won't rust)

* A strip of rubber (car inner tube is good) 15cm long and thick enough to attach the roof to the back of the nest-box

* A pencil

* A ruler

Mark out the wood with sawing lines as shown in the diagram. Saw along the dotted lines to produce the roof, the back, the front, two sides and the floor.

If you are making a small-hole nest-box, drill a hole in the front panel. An entrance hole 28mm in diameter will suit birds such as blue tits, great tits, coal tits, tree sparrows and pied flycatchers. A slightly larger hole of 32mm will also attract house sparrows, nuthatches and lesser spotted woodpeckers.

To make an open-fronted nest box, saw the front panel in half from side to side, so that the top half of the front is completely open.

Nail together the sides, the front and the floor. Attach the roof to the back using the rubber strip, which becomes a hinge to lift open the lid when you need to clean the nest-box. Drill small holes in the bottom to let water drain away.

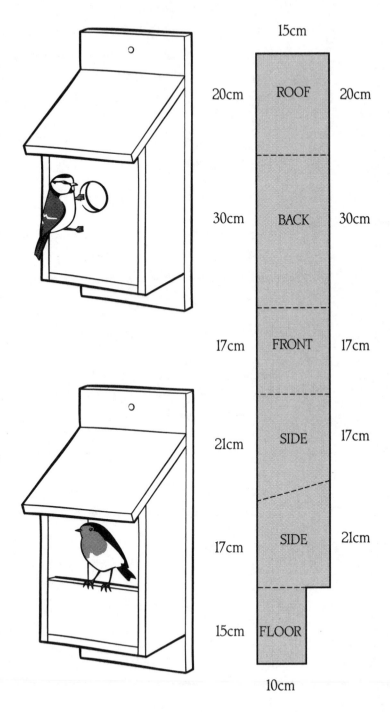

15cm

20cm	ROOF	20cm
30cm	BACK	30cm
17cm	FRONT	17cm
21cm	SIDE	17cm
17cm	SIDE	21cm
15cm	FLOOR	

10cm

WHERE TO PUT NEST-BOXES

You can attach nest-boxes to trees or walls, making sure that they are high enough off the ground to be safe from inquisitive cats. The front should face somewhere between south-east and north; this shelters it from strong direct sunlight and the heaviest rain.

Don't put nest-boxes close to a bird-table or feeding area, because the constant coming and going of many other birds could well prevent breeding.

WINTER CLEANING

When the breeding season has finished, nest-boxes should be taken down and cleaned. Insist that the whole family joins in, removing old nesting material (remember to wear gloves) and carefully scalding the inside of the box with boiling water to kill any parasites.

UNHATCHED EGGS

If there are any unhatched eggs in the box, the law says that they can only be removed between October and January. Even if the family want to keep the eggs, they have to be destroyed; keeping unhatched eggs is illegal.

WINTER SHELTER

Once a box has been emptied and cleaned, check that there are no gaps where the wooden pieces join and that the roof still fits properly. Then put it back in place, so that it can give birds a roosting place in bad weather.

WHAT NOT TO DO AT FAMILY GATHERINGS

Bad behaviour when staying with relatives still counts as bad behaviour, even though they are technically 'family'. The following things are simply unacceptable and deserve a red card ...

* Occupying the most comfortable chair in the room all the time.

* Never offering to help in the kitchen and, when asked, saying you don't want to get in the way.

* Taking your own supply of loo paper and leaving it beside the roll provided, where everyone can see it.

* Implying that your hosts' cooking isn't up to much and offering to take them out to dinner at a notoriously seedy pub.

* Telling your hosts to sit down and relax when they are rushed off their feet trying to entertain you.

* Demanding a large brandy when you are asked if you would like anything with your morning coffee. (When you are offered milk and sugar, refusing them with a look of disgust.)

* Sitting in front of the fire and keeping the heat from other people.

* Interrupting other people and making it obvious that you think what they are saying is boring.

* Repeatedly asking close relatives to tell you who they are because you're 'hopeless with names'.

* Making rude remarks to people about relatives who you know are on their side of the family.

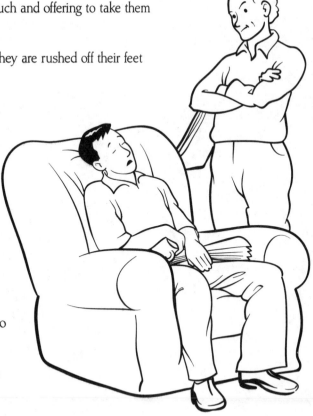

How To Wash A Dog In Space

Dogs travelled in space before human beings, but you don't really hear about space dogs any more. Perhaps this is because those early space flights were much shorter than modern space missions. Present-day space flights last so long that a space dog would start to smell. The astronauts would have to give the dog a bath and that could prove to be quite difficult. In space, where there is no gravity, the dog, the water, the bottle of dog shampoo, the towel – everything in fact – would float about inside the spacecraft.

RETURN OF THE SPACE DOGS

There may come a time, though, when dogs will need to be washed in space. Space experts talk of people travelling to other planets on journeys lasting several years. Their dogs will miss them and they will miss their dogs. So the dogs will have to go on the missions as well.

What about people who go to live on the moon? They will want their pets for company, won't they? One way or another, dogs will be travelling in space. They'll need to be washed and a way of doing that will have to be invented. Here's one suggestion.

THE INTERGALACTIC DOGGIE-DOUCHE

One of the problems of washing anything in space, never mind a dog with a thick coat which likes to shake itself dry, is that water floats everywhere. This can be dangerous if it lands on electrical appliances and spacecraft are lined with electronic equipment. To be safe, then, the Intergalactic Doggie-Douche (IDD) will be housed in a plastic tent. You and the dog will float inside and zip it closed, to keep all the water away from the rest of the spacecraft.

HIGH AND DRY

You will fasten your dog's collar to a lead fixed inside the IDD, to stop it trying to run away from the water; in fact, because the IDD is weightless, the dog will be floating and won't be able to run. You will be wearing a waterproof suit and special IDD helmet, so the water won't affect you. There will be a hose with a sprinkler (like a shower head on earth), which you will use to wash the dog. Unlike dog-washing on earth, however, the IDD will have a vacuum hose to suck up the used water.

When the dog is washed, you will be able to use the third piece of equipment in the IDD – a dog-sized hair-dryer. Trying to rub a dog dry with a towel is hard work in space, because you and the dog will keep drifting away from each other. A hair-dryer is more efficient and much easier to use. Once the dog is clean, dry and smelling nice once again, you'll give it a hug and a pat – and don't forget a little doggie treat. Dogs enjoy those wherever they are.

CREATE SPECTACULAR SUMS

These sums look amazing when you present them to people. Try them out on the family to begin with. If you want to appear to be a real genius, sit them round while you write out a sum and watch their reactions.

$$1 \times 9 + 9 = 18$$
$$12 \times 9 + 9 = 117$$
$$123 \times 9 + 9 = 1116$$
$$1234 \times 9 + 9 = 11115$$
$$12345 \times 9 + 9 = 111114$$
$$123456 \times 9 + 9 = 1111113$$
$$1234567 \times 9 + 9 = 11111112$$
$$12345678 \times 9 + 9 = 111111111$$

$$1 \times 9 - 1 = 8$$
$$21 \times 9 - 1 = 188$$
$$321 \times 9 - 1 = 2888$$
$$4321 \times 9 - 1 = 38888$$
$$54321 \times 9 - 1 = 488888$$
$$654321 \times 9 - 1 = 5888888$$
$$7654321 \times 9 - 1 = 68888888$$
$$87654321 \times 9 - 1 = 788888888$$
$$987654321 \times 9 - 1 = 8888888888$$

MAKE APPLE-PIE BEDS

As simple practical jokes go, this is a sure-fire winner. It's easy to prepare and always catches people out when they're getting into bed and least expecting someone to pull a trick on them. Unfortunately you need sheets and blankets to make it work properly – duvets simply don't achieve the same effect.

BED MAKING WITH A DIFFERENCE

An apple-pie bed looks like any other bed – it's only when you try to get down inside that you discover that your legs won't fit, because a sheet has been doubled back on itself. Here's how to make it:

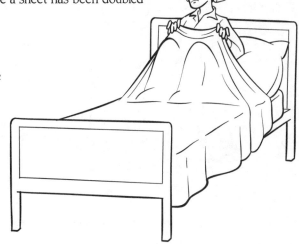

1 Strip the bed clothes.

2 Tuck the bottom sheet under the pillow end of the mattress as usual.

3 But, instead of tucking the other end under the mattress at the foot of the bed, fold it halfway down the bed and pull the free end up to the pillow.

4 Now place the blankets and quilt on the bed as you normally would and tuck them in as usual.

5 Fold the free end of the bottom sheet from the pillow over the quilt and blankets and tuck it in, so that it looks like the folded and tucked top sheet.

6 There – your apple-pie bed is ready.

7 Now wait for the unsuspecting victim to try to get into it.

Like all practical jokes, this works best when used sparingly. And in case you want to know why it is called an 'apple-pie bed', the explanation probably has something to do with the French *nappe pliée*, meaning a 'folded sheet' or 'folded cloth'.

MAKE MONEY FROM THINGS YOU NO LONGER NEED

Most families build up a collection of things they no longer need or no longer use. Clothes are outgrown or go out of fashion. CDs and DVDs lose their interest as well. Things get pushed to the back of cupboards and drawers all over the house. The loft, the garage and the garden shed become general dumping grounds.

Just because your family no longer needs these things doesn't mean they won't be of interest to other people. They could start to interest you quite a bit too, if you were able to make money out of them.

FOR SALE

You have to decide the best place to advertise things you want to sell. Obviously there is no point spending a lot of money to advertise something worth much less. However, you may have some things you no longer need that are worth quite a lot of money to other people. There are specialist collectors of so many different things, so any 'antiques' dating from Mum and Dad's childhood or teenage years should be looked at carefully before being disposed of.

OUTLETS

* Local shops will often let you place 'For Sale' notices in the window for a small fee.

* Even some supermarkets will let you display small cards to sell things, though you must check with staff first.

✳ Many local newspapers let you advertise a wide range of things for free.

✳ Specialist shops that sell items like bicycles, musical instruments and sports equipment have display boards where you can advertise similar goods for sale.

✳ There are also shops that sell second-hand goods. They might be interested in things you have for sale: items of furniture, for example.

✳ Some shops buy computer games, CDs and DVDs that are still in good condition.

✳ If you have access to the internet (and Mum and Dad must set up the ID and deal with the actual selling) there are web sites where people buy things from other people. A site like eBay lets people all over the world buy and sell things on-line.

WORDS OF WARNING

✳ It's never a good idea to sell things to people you know. So don't try and pass on your old toys, CDs, games or DVDs to friends *unless* everyone in both families agrees to it.

✳ Most schools don't allow pupils to buy and sell things to each other at school. There are plenty of other places to try.

✳ Let everyone in the family see your advertisement *before* it goes on display, or is sent to a newspaper. Someone may prefer you to change the details: for example, to ask people to telephone at certain times of the day, when they know someone will be at home.

✳ Why not have a garage sale? Never try to sell things on the street – you will probably be breaking the law if you do.

Ways To Avoid Being Struck By Lightning

The odds against being killed by lightning are about 1 in 19,000,000. However, Dad needs to watch out because four out of five lightning deaths in the last 50 years have been men. Experts also estimate that there are 100 lightning flashes around the world every second – that's an average of 8,640,000 every day. Therefore, it's probably a good idea for all the family to know exactly what to do in a thunderstorm.

DANGER! DANGER!

As a rule of thumb if you can hear thunder you are in striking distance of lightning. The shorter the time delay between hearing a crash of thunder and seeing the flash of lightning, the closer you are to the storm. If your family is sensible, you won't hang around to find out how far away the storm is. Lightning bolts can be five times hotter than the surface of the sun!

BE INSIDE – BE SAFE

There's no question about it, being indoors is far safer in a thunderstorm than being outside. Even so, you need to take care. Stay away from electrical equipment. It's also advisable to unplug electrical appliances because lightning can cause power surges. Keep away from surfaces that might conduct electricity, such as metal windows, the sink, the shower – in fact stay away from plumbing altogether (the metal pipes can conduct electricity).

OUT IN THE OPEN

If the family is caught out in the open you need to reduce the risk of attracting lightning. Look for somewhere low-lying – away from metal fences, power cables, poles or trees. People need to make themselves as small as possible and reduce contact with the ground. This means that the family should spread out rather than huddling together. Each person should crouch down and balance on the balls of their feet. They should put their hands on their knees and tuck their head between them. Not easy!

No one should use a mobile phone or put up an umbrella – the metal could act as a lightning conductor.

If you can't find shelter (a metal shed is *not* a good choice), then a vehicle is a safe alternative. Pile in and close the windows. No one should touch the doors, windows, roof, gear stick, handbrake or steering wheel. If lightning does strike the car, the electrical charge will pass round the metal frame and out through the tyres.

If your family is out in a boat, row for the shore for all you are worth as soon as a thunderstorm is spotted.

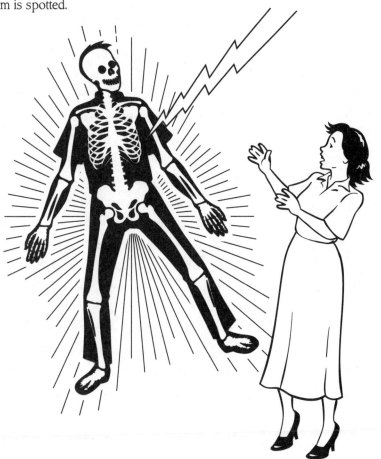

What To Do In A Minefield

Unless the people next door are seriously nasty and bury mines round the outside of their garden to keep out intruders, families will only wander into minefields when they are visiting other countries. Sadly there are countries in many parts of the world where minefields exist: in Africa, Asia, the Middle East and in Europe. So people need to be careful when they are walking in countries where there has been fighting. Even if the fighting was as far back as 20 years ago, minefields might not have been cleared and the mines will still be active and very, very dangerous.

TIPS TO AVOID MINEFIELDS

The safest way for people to protect themselves from being blown up by mines is not to stray into a minefield in the first place. Mum and Dad might be carried away with the scenery. They might want to go closer to a beautiful plant to look at the flowers, or nearer a building to take a better picture. But other people in the family

can check for warning signs.

Sometimes there will be a notice saying something like 'Danger – Mines'. So it's useful to learn the local word for a 'mine'. Though any sign with a skull and crossed bones is a good clue. Ask local people if there are mines (another good reason for learning the local language). See where the locals walk. If they avoid particular tracks and trails, it could be because they are mined. Your family should avoid them as well.

Everyone can help check where they are walking. Shallow bumps and signs that the soil has been disturbed can mean that mines have been buried there. Wires stretched across paths and tracks are warnings too. These are tripwires, which explode mines when people catch their feet in them.

BACKING OUT TO SAFETY

Any member of the family who is unfortunate enough (or careless enough) to walk into a minefield needs to stay very cool when they discover where they are. Maybe a mine will explode in the distance because an animal has trodden on it. Or a strange-looking spike sticking out of the ground will be the clue. Whatever happens, everyone needs to stop walking immediately and look at their feet.

They shouldn't turn round. If there are no unusual shapes in the ground beside their feet they should back up slowly, retracing their steps exactly by placing their feet in their own footprints. They must keep walking backwards very carefully, looking where their feet are going all the time. Only when they are sure that they are on safe ground can they stop. Next time (and everyone will be sure there *won't* be a next time) they'll know better.

HAVE A HAND SHADOW COMPETITION

You can create magical effects at home with the contrast between light and shadow. With a little practice you can use your hands and fingers to cast shadows and create an entertaining family competition. All you need is a source of light that throws a strong beam – a desk lamp or a powerful torch would be ideal – and a blank wall.

You can either divide the family into teams, or you can play as individuals. The team or player who correctly identifies the most hand shadows is the winner.

To get you started, here are some hand-shadows to practise and to give you ideas for making shapes of your own.

Try creating ...

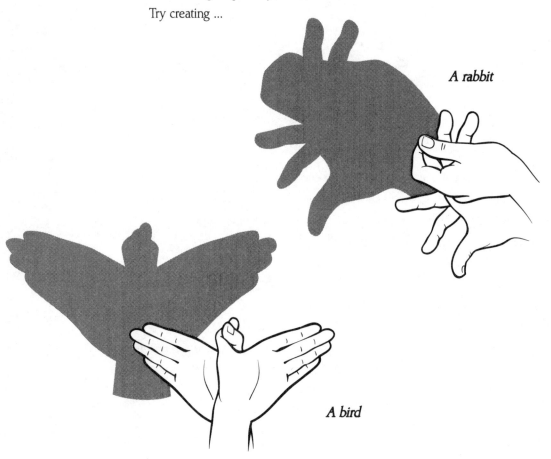

A rabbit

A bird

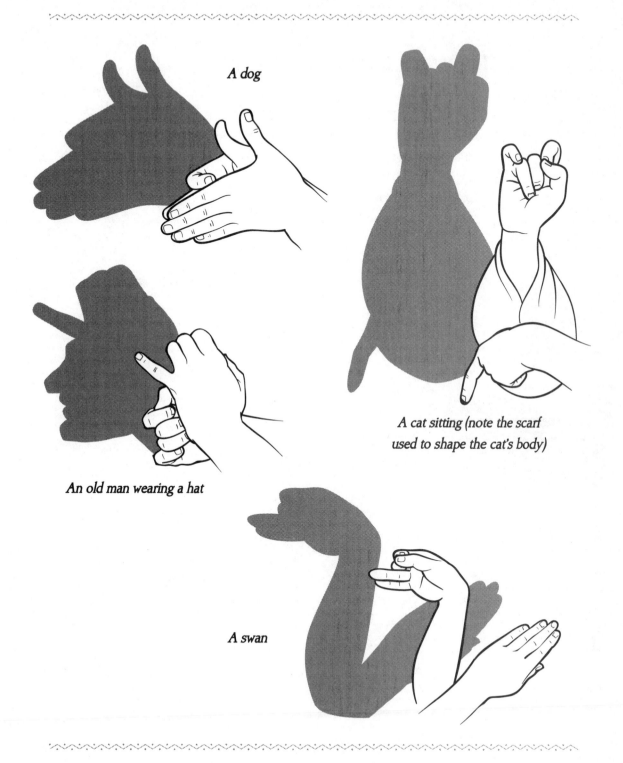

A dog

A cat sitting (note the scarf used to shape the cat's body)

An old man wearing a hat

A swan

HOW TO LIVE FOREVER

No one alive today has any idea what science and medicine may discover in centuries to come. We are used to people living for close to a hundred years (or longer in some exceptional cases), but in the distant future people of a hundred might be considered quite young.

However, there are some people who have thought about what might happen and decided to take steps to make sure they are around hundreds of years from now, so that they can experience the future and possibly be given amazing new medical treatments as well.

So how do they choose to do this? The simple answer is by deep-freezing. The scientific name for this: cryonics.

FROZEN IN TIME

* As soon as the person wanting to be preserved is declared dead, they are frozen in liquid nitrogen.

* This acts so quickly on their body that very little decay takes place.

* Instead, the body is preserved in perfect condition and it is stored like this for as long as necessary. That's the idea at least. A lot of people are doubtful whether the process will actually work and whether human bodies can really be preserved by deep freezing.

BACK TO THE FUTURE

* People who believe their bodies can be stored in this way hope that doctors in the future will find ways to cure whatever made them die.

* They also believe that science will have found a way of thawing their frozen bodies and bringing them back to life, so that they can be 'cured' and even be made younger.

* Be warned, this is a lot to expect from scientists and doctors, and no one can promise that it will succeed.

* Still, if you have £75,000 to spare when you are very old and aren't in too much of a hurry, one day you could live forever.

Boxing Clever

By copying the board below on to a sheet of paper (the dots only), two people can play this game in a car, train or plane, or during a quiet moment at home.

Players will need something to write with.

BOXED IN

* The aim of the game is to complete as many 'boxes' as possible, but each player can only draw one line joining two dots each go.

* A box is completed by drawing the fourth side of a square after the other three sides have been drawn.

* Clearly players should try to avoid drawing the third side of a box, to prevent their opponents scoring easy points.

* When a player completes a box they draw another line and write their initials inside the completed box.

* So it's possible for a player to complete several boxes in one go – their turn only ends when they draw a line that does not complete a box.

* Play ends when all the boxes have been completed. The player with the greater number of boxes is the winner.

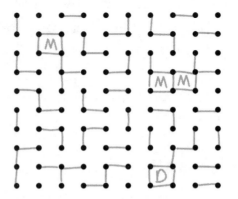

DOODLING IN THE DARK

There may be doubts about how good at drawing certain members of the family are before they try their hand at this, but afterwards there will be no doubts at all. This is why . . .

* Everyone has paper, pencil and a blindfold.

* You all put on your blindfolds. Pick up your pencils and position these over your sheets of paper (if you're lucky).

* Now that everyone is ready, you each have to draw a picture of a house.

* When this is completed, you have to draw a garden in front of your house.

* Then some trees behind it.

* Next, some clouds in the sky.

* A car parked on a road in front of the garden.

* The last piece of the drawing is a dog, in the garden.

* Only when all the drawings are completed is everyone allowed to remove their blindfolds and inspect their masterpieces.

* Then look at what everyone else has drawn and fall about laughing!

HEARTBREAK HOTEL

The family checks into a hotel and heads down to the hotel restaurant. There's a bellboy sitting in the corner of the restaurant scratching his head. He has a mathematical problem and needs help. Who in your family can work out his problem?

CLERICAL ERROR

Earlier that day three guests checked into a room in the hotel. The desk clerk told them the room was £30, so each man paid £10 and went to the room. A while later the desk clerk realised he had made a mistake. The room was only £25, so he called the bellboy over. He gave the bellboy five pound coins and sent him off to the men's room to refund them.

On the way to the room, the bellboy realised he couldn't figure out how to split the £5 evenly between the three men, so when he knocked at the door he gave each man £1 and kept the other £2 for himself as a tip.

BRAIN BUSTER

This means that the men each paid £9 for the room, which is a total of £27. If you add the £2 that the bellboy kept, that makes £29.

Who has the other pound?
Can anyone figure it out?
You'll find the answer on page 188.

WHERE DOES THE TIME GO?

How often do you hear people saying they don't know where the time goes? How often does someone in the family complain that they spend too long at work or at school? It's time to put a stop to these gross exaggerations.

If you want to know where the time really goes, take a look at this chart, which shows that people only spend *one* day a year at work or school.

Amazing isn't it?

These are the reasons why:

✳ Each year has	365 days
✳ Each day we spend 8 hours sleeping	– 122 days
	243 days
✳ Each day we have about 8 hours leisure	– 122 days
	121 days
✳ Subtract 52 Sundays in the year	– 52 days
	69 days
✳ Subtract 12 hours a week (spent travelling to work/school and for 'unofficial' breaks)	– 26 days
	43 days
✳ Subtract daily average of 1 hour 50 minutes for lunch, breaks, time off work/school	– 28 days
	15 days
✳ Subtract two weeks' holiday	– 14 days
✳ Leaving	1 day

BUILD AN EMERGENCY SHELTER IN THE FOREST

Imagine for a moment that your family is lost in a forest and that it will be dark in two hours' time. You have food and warm clothes. Safe drinking water is nearby. The only things you don't have are tents and any way of contacting rescuers. What should you do?

You might be tempted to keep on walking, hoping you will find a road or a hut before it gets dark. The safest thing to do, though, is to use the remaining daylight to build a shelter for the night. In that way your family can be sure of having somewhere warm and dry to rest until morning.

THE NEST BEST THING

One of the few good points about being lost in a forest is that there is plenty of building material all around. Branches, leaves, moss and grass can all be used to make a cosy shelter. Birds build their nests using material like this – all your family needs to do is build 'nests' that you can shelter in.

It probably isn't practical to make a shelter for everyone to get in; finding enough material of the right size would take too long. A better plan is to build shelters that two people can fit inside: one for Dad and one of the kids, maybe, the other for Mum and the fourth member of the family.

The shelters can be built close together, and they can be built at the same time, so no daylight is wasted.

LAYER BY LAYER

The first part of the simple forest shelter to look for is a long pole or a small fallen tree. This needs to be between one and a half and two times the height of the tallest person going inside the shelter.

Now the family needs to find something that can support one end of the pole, which will act as the main beam of the shelter. A large rock would do. So would a tree stump, or a tree with a forked branch. Whatever you choose, the support needs to be slightly taller than the tallest person when he or she is sitting.

Once the main beam is propped in place, smaller poles are placed on either side to make a framework shaped like a tent. Place the poles close together and fill the gaps between them with smaller branches.

When this first layer is completed, you'll need to cover it with whatever you can find to act as insulation. Dead leaves, dry ferns, grass, moss, evergreen branches – anything like that can be piled on top of the frame until there is a thick layer.

The final layer is made of light branches placed over the outside of the shelter to prevent the insulating material from blowing away.

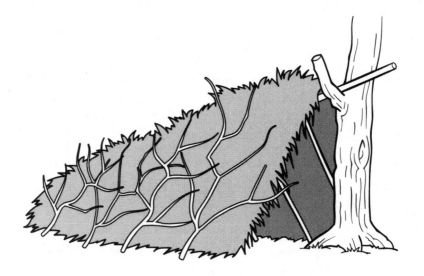

HOME FROM HOME

It makes sense to use the same support for both shelters. The entrances can face each other by the support, while the shelters slope away in opposite directions.

When the outside structure is complete, both shelters will need a layer of comfortable material to lie on inside. This needs to be at least 30cm thick because your body can lose heat very quickly if you lie on bare ground.

The final part of the structure is a pile of insulating material near the entrance which can be used to block out cold air when the people are tucked up inside.

If gathering material and building the shelters is well organised, both should be ready by the time darkness falls. Your family will be snug and safe, and much happier than if they were wandering around a cold dark forest all night.

HAVE A MATCHBOX RACE

If your family is looking for a fun game to play with all the relatives at Christmas they don't need to look any further. This game doesn't take a lot of skill, it only needs two matchbox covers and guarantees lots of laughs.

WINNING BY A NOSE

To have a Matchbox Race, the family divides into two teams, with an equal number of players on each team. One of the players in each team has a matchbox cover and on the word 'Go' they push their matchbox covers over their noses, so that they can be transferred nose to nose between the rest of the team.

Players aren't allowed to touch the matchbox cover with their hands and if any player does touch it, or drops the matchbox cover on the floor, it has to be returned to the first player who must begin the passing sequence all over again.

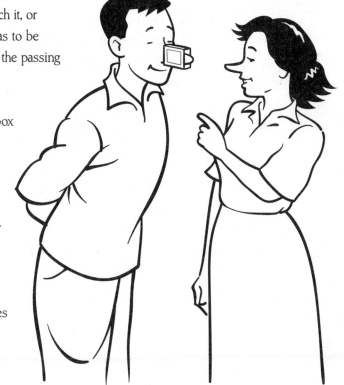

If there are more than four players in a team, they form a line and pass the matchbox cover nose to nose down the line and back to the first player. The first team to finish this wins.

If there are fewer players in a team, the challenge is to pass the matchbox cover between the players six times. The same rules about not touching and not dropping the matchbox apply and the first team that passes the matchbox nose to nose six times is the winner. If you believe in Pinocchio, it might be a good idea to do some serious fibbing before the competition!

How To Stick Pins In Balloons Without Bursting Them

Stick a pin in a balloon and what happens? It bursts with a loud bang. Everyone knows that.

Steady, though ... there is a way of sticking a pin into a balloon (an inflated balloon) without it bursting.

This is a good test of family brain power and cunning.

1 So, give everyone a balloon.

2 Get them to blow up their balloons and tie the ends so the air inside doesn't escape.

3 Now give each person a pin and see who can come up with a way of pushing the pin through the tight skin of the balloon without producing a loud bang and a small piece of limp rubber. Tell them they can use anything in the house to help them.

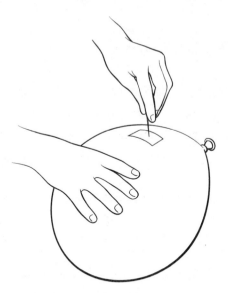

There is a way of doing this and, if no one has guessed, it involves using sticky tape.

4 Cut a small piece of tape.

5 Position it anywhere on the balloon.

6 Make sure the tape is stuck down securely.

7 Now try to force a pin through the area covered by tape and into the balloon.

8 The first thing you'll notice is that there *isn't* a loud bang, because the balloon hasn't popped.

9 The only noise you'll hear will be a hissing sound made by air escaping through the small hole made by the pin.

Eventually the balloon will become deflated, but it will lose air like a bicycle tyre with a puncture – not in one big pop. The sticky tape is stronger than the 'skin' of the balloon, so it's able to stop the pin prick growing into a larger hole and causing a bang.

If you use a transparent tape, no one will know that it isn't an ordinary balloon that you are trying to pop – magic!

WRITE INVISIBLE MESSAGES

Suppose a blank sheet of paper turns up in the post one day, or you come home and find it lying on the kitchen table. In most families it would probably be thrown away – but then most families might not suspect that the paper with no writing on it actually contains an invisible message. What a brilliant way of keeping things secret in the family!

Here are two techniques using things most people have at home.

WAXING LYRICAL

1 For this kind of secret writing you will need: a white candle, a thin sheet of paper, a sheet of normal writing paper and a writing instrument made from a piece of sharpened wood, such as a cocktail stick.

2 Rub candle wax all over one side of the thin paper.

3 Place the thin paper, waxed-side down, on the sheet of writing paper.

4 Write your message by printing firmly. This will leave the message on the writing paper *but* because the message will be in wax, no one will know it is there. The paper will appear to be blank.

5 When the writing paper is received, the person it has been sent to needs to sprinkle it with some powder. Talcum powder would work well, as would instant coffee powder.

7. After sprinkling the powder, give the writing paper a gentle shake. Most of the powder will slide off the paper, but the hidden message will now be visible, because some of the dust will have stuck to the wax.

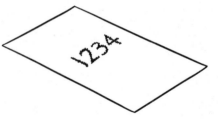

POTATO INK

1. This form of invisible writing is even easier because all you need is a thin sheet of paper, a potato, a flat-bladed knife and a sharpened wooden writing instrument as before.

2. Cut the potato in half and scoop a hole in one of the cut sides.

3. Use the knife blade to scrape and squeeze juice from the cut surface into the hole you have made.

4. Using the hole as an inkwell, dip the writing stick into it, collecting some juice on the end, and write out your message with the juice.

5. When the 'ink' dries your message will disappear.

6. To make the message reappear, it needs to be heated up. You could hold it beside a warm radiator, or place it in a warm oven. You should *never* hold it in front of a naked flame, like a candle or a fire, in case the paper suddenly catches fire itself.

7. As the paper warms, the message will appear again, so that it can be read.

BUMPER STICKERS NOT TO PUT ON THE FAMILY CAR

Some bumper stickers carry positive, uplifting messages that inspire people who read them to see the world in a better light. Some don't.

These fall into the second category and are best left off your family car:

✳ Yes – I do own the road.

✳ It matters not if you win or lose. It only matters that I win.

✳ If all else fails, stop using all else.

✳ If this sticker is getting smaller, the light is probably green.

✳ Hell was full, so I came back.

How To Make A Toy That Really Works From Junk And Rubbish

The family picnic is over and now you discover that someone has forgotten to pack any of the outdoor games you meant to bring. No problem. If you've two or more large plastic bottles, paper and a knife or scissors, it won't take long to make something you can enjoy playing with and improve your catching skills at the same time.

BOTTLE CATCH

1. Carefully cut the bottoms off the plastic bottles, so that they each measure about 25cm from the neck.

2. Now cut out a section like the one shown below and remember to cut curved corners, so that there are no sharp edges.

3. Crunch up the paper to make a ball. If you have any sticky tape, wrap this round to keep the ball tight. (You could use string, or fishing line, secured with a knot if you don't have sticky tape.) If you want the ball to have more weight, wrap the paper round a pebble, making sure that it's well padded.

4. Now you have catchers and a ball, which you can use to create your own game.

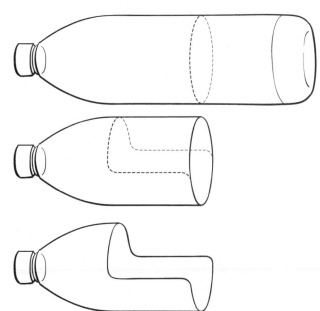

Family Facial Olympics

On your marks. Get set. Go!

It's time for the games to begin – though with these Olympic games you don't have to have a stadium or any equipment. All you need is your face, a watch or clock, which shows seconds as well as minutes and hours, and spectators (who also act as judges).

THE CHALLENGE

Like many Olympic events, this calls for skill, agility and speed, rather than strength. You can compete in any position that suits you – sitting down, lying down or standing up. As long as the spectators/judges can see your face, that's all that matters.

Each competitor has to perform every one of the movements set down by the judges, in the correct order and as fast as they can. A penalty of five seconds is added to their time for each movement that is out of sequence, or which is incorrectly performed. Before competing, each competitor should be given a piece of paper showing the order in which the movements have to be made. The judges will have the same sheet and all competitors will perform the movements in the same order.

THE EVENT

You can organise your own competition around these movements. You can place them in any order you like and repeat them as often as you want. Remember, it's not winning that counts, but taking part. (And it might be worth reminding the more competitive people in the family about this before the games begin!)

1. Close left eye.
2. Close right eye.
3. Close both eyes.
4. Open mouth.
5. Smile.
6. Wiggle nose from side to side.
7. Move nose to left.
8. Move nose to right.
9. Raise right eyebrow, if you can.
10. Raise left eyebrow, if you can.
11. Raise both eyebrows.
12. Place tongue over top lip.
13. Place tongue over bottom lip.
14. Stick out flat tongue.
15. Stick out rolled tongue.
16. Point tongue to left of mouth.
17. Point tongue to right of mouth.
18. Press tongue against inside of left cheek.
19. Press tongue against inside of right cheek.
20. Combine any two of the above to create another movement.

DRAWING THE IMPOSSIBLE

Put the family's practical skills to the test with this 'Mission Impossible'. First show everyone these pictures then close the book and see who can draw them correctly.

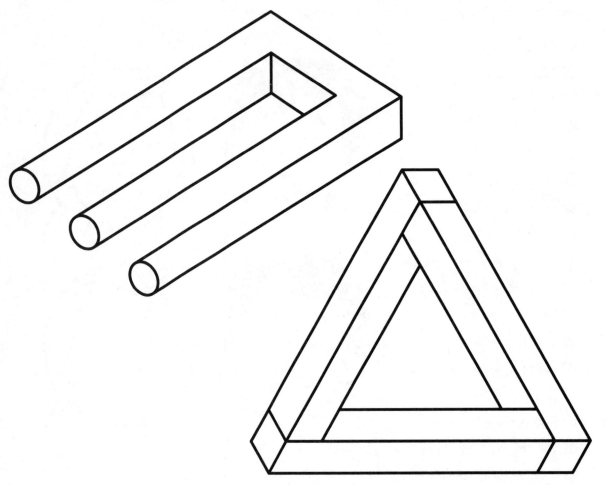

Then see who can discover a way of making them. Just so that you don't waste too much of your time, you should know that these objects are optical illusions and can never be constructed, even though they can be drawn. But keep this fact hidden from sight until the rest of the family gives up.

QUARTER A CIRCLE WITH THREE EQUAL LINES

Dividing a circle into three equal parts using three lines of equal length is very easy, as this diagram shows.

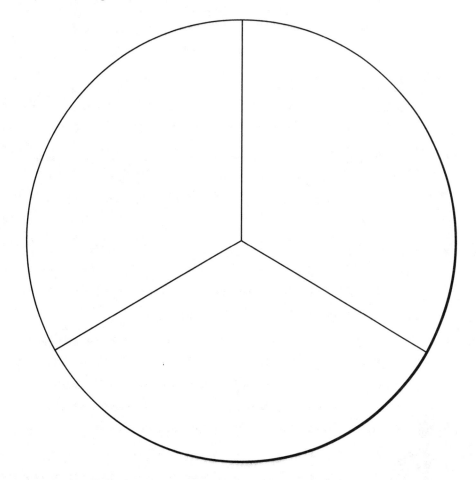

However, the family will have some head scratching to do when asked to divide a circle into *four* equal parts, but still using just three lines of equal length. The lines don't have to be straight, but they must not cross. The answer is on page 188.

How To Convince People You Are A Family Of Vampires

You don't actually have to go round sucking blood from victims to give people the impression yours is a freaky family. There are subtler ways of getting across the message that there's something decidedly dead about you all.

MEET THE VAMPIRES

* At night, under the cover of darkness, vampires leave their graves to walk abroad. Make sure no one in your family is seen outside the house in daylight. Word will soon get around that you are a strange bunch.

* Traditionally vampires are corpses that have returned from the grave to haunt the living. So when you *are* seen, be sure that you all have sickly pale skin that has not seen sunlight for a very long time (use make-up or, failing that, talcum powder).

* Vampires suck blood from their victims, because human blood is what keeps vampires 'alive'. The neck is their favourite sucking spot. So show an unnatural interest in people's necks – try admiring a piece of jewellery perhaps, or asking men if they nicked themselves shaving that morning.

* Vampires have sharp fangs through which they suck blood from their victims' necks. Never let people see your teeth. Make a point of keeping your mouth closed or covering it with your hand when you laugh or cough. You could even persuade Dad to smear ketchup around his mouth and pretend to wipe it away guiltily when spotted.

* Vampires have the power to hypnotise their victims during an attack, so they never remember the vampire draining their blood from them. Practise and perfect the art of gazing at people with an unblinking stare – guaranteed to unnerve the neighbours.

✳ Make sure everyone in the family always wears black. Capes are an excellent touch and a vampire fashion must.

✳ According to traditional beliefs vampires can be frightened away by garlic, wild roses, crucifixes and fire. Maybe Mum can flinch when she passes garlic in the supermarket aisle, or Dad can back away from the barbecue looking fearful.

REVAMP YOUR HOUSE

In the unlikely event anyone comes by to visit you at home (and such visits will soon stop completely once word spreads) you need to make some changes to the house. Keep all curtains closed, and plenty of candles burning. Have a few long wooden boxes with open lids on view. Visitors will think your house is scary as

soon as they step inside. They will think the wooden boxes are coffins. Vampires lie in coffins when they return from stalking the neighbourhood. So frightened visitors will quickly think that your family lies around in coffins during the day – and this will confirm their suspicions that you are a family of vampires.

NEIGHBOURS FROM HELL

If you've just moved to a new house, it's easier to convince the neighbours that you're all vampires. Failing that, tell your neighbours you're going on holiday to Transylvania (where the notorious vampire, Count Dracula, once terrified the locals). Behaving strangely after you get home should be quite enough to convince anyone that you've been bitten by the best.

How To Be The First To Reach 100

This game is all about being the first to reach 100 when you take it in turns counting with someone else. Doesn't sound that difficult, does it?

THE RULES

1 The person who starts chooses any single-figure number.
2 The other player follows by adding any number between 1 and 10.
3 Play continues in this way, with the players taking it in turn to add numbers between 1 and 10 to the total.
4 The winner is the player who reaches 100 first.

HOW IT WORKS

The game seems quite simple. However, unless you understand how it works, you can never be sure that you will win. Check out the tips below and you'll discover that there is a definite knack that needs to be learnt if you want to be sure of winning.

* It's clear that the winner will be the person who makes his or her opponent reach 99, because the only number after that in the game is 100.

* If one player reaches 89 before the other, that player has also won, because the largest number the second player can reach is 99 (89 + 10 = 99).

* To reach 89, a player also needs to be the first to 78, for the same reasons.

* Continuing along these lines, the winning player must also be the first to reach 67, 56, 45, 34, 23 and 12.

* So, the game is virtually over once a player (who understands the secret) reaches 12.

* In fact, anyone who starts with a number other than 1 will always be beaten by a player who knows the secret, because adding any number between 1 and 10 will reach 12 on the winning player's first go.

SURVIVE A VOLCANIC ERUPTION

Just about the last thing anyone needs on a hiking holiday in fabulous scenery is to hear rumbling and feel the ground starting to shake. It's not last night's supper getting its own back. This is serious. This is a volcano getting ready to erupt!

THINK AND BE SAFE

Several dangers will follow the rumbling and shaking.

Rocks and debris may start tumbling down the side of the volcano. If the family is in their path, Mum and Dad need to crouch in a ball, backs to the falling debris and protect their heads with their hands. If the kids are small enough, they should crouch in the same positions, in front of Mum and Dad, whose bodies will shelter them.

If there is lava flowing towards them, your family must get out of its path as soon as possible. You won't be able to outrun it, so running downhill is no good. If there's a valley or depression that might divert the lava, try to get across to the safe side.

The best plan is to get indoors and move to a higher floor. All doors and windows should be closed to keep out dangerous fumes and gases. Some of these fumes and gases do not have strong odours and aren't easy to detect. Some are heavier than air and collect at floor level, which is why people should stand up, not sit or lie on the floor.

If there is enough time your family should get to a car and, if the authorities are telling people to evacuate the area, drive well away until the threat has passed. But don't let Dad think he can pretend to be a rally driver and outpace a lava flow. Some can travel much faster than he will be able to drive. That's why people need to think first to be sure of being safe when an eruption begins.

How To Find Underground Water By Dowsing

For centuries people have been discovering water underground by dowsing for it and to this day no one can explain how, or why, they are able to do it. Some people maintain that being able to dowse successfully is some kind of mystical gift. Others don't believe in it at all. Whatever people believe, it is a useful skill for making sure no one steps in the puddle the puppy left or, if the family fancy a fine water feature, for finding a natural spring in the garden.

EQUIPMENT

Dowsers traditionally used forked hazel branches. More technically minded dowsers prefer L-shaped rods made of copper or iron. However, a wire coat hangers can work just as well – if you have the 'gift'.

To make a pair of dowsing rods you'll need two wire coat hangers. Using wire cutters, make a cut at one end of the long horizontal length (the one that a pair of trousers might hang over). Then make the second cut about 10cm up from the angled end in the direction of the hook at the top of the coat hanger.

Repeat this with the second hanger, so that you have matching pieces of wire. Bend each of the short lengths until they make an L-shape. These are your dowsing rods, with the short lengths acting as handles. Slip half a plastic drinking straw over each handle, so that the rod can swivel freely when you hold it.

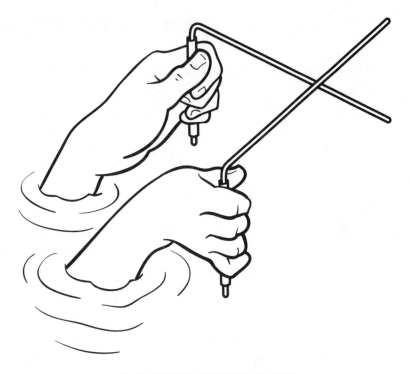

DOWSING TECHNIQUE

1 Hold a rod in each hand, horizontally in front of you, pointing forwards.

2 Walk steadily over the ground where you think underground water might be running.

3 When you find the water, the rods will cross each other.

4 Stop walking and ask someone in the family to mark the spot on the ground where the rods have crossed.

5 Now let someone else have a turn and watch to see if the rods cross for them over the same place.

6 If they do, the family could develop a useful sideline in finding water for paying customers.

How To Find Any Word In Any Book

This looks like a brilliant piece of mind-reading when really it's a simple piece of maths (although using a calculator will speed it up). So, you can show your family that you're a genuine genius and a maths marvel at the same time. That can't be bad.

WORD SEARCH

Ask someone in the family to open any book they choose at any page.

Ask them to select a word on that page, *but* they must not tell anyone else what that word is, or where it appears in the book.

Explain that you are going to use a secret mathematical formula to identify that particular word, the page it is on and exactly where on that page it is printed! There will be thousands of words in the book and everyone will think you're boasting. But you'll soon prove them wrong.

CUNNING CALCULATIONS

1. Hand a calculator to the person who selected the secret word.

2. Ask them to multiply the page number by 100.

3. Next ask them to add 25.

4. Now get them to count down the lines from the top of the page until they reach the line where the secret word appears.

5. They add the number they have just counted.

6. The total showing on the calculator must now be multiplied by 100.

7 Now ask them to count along the words in the line until they reach their chosen word.

8 The number of the word is now added.

9 That's the end of the calculation. Ask what the total is and say that this is all you need to pinpoint the word and where it appears in the book.

10 Ask for the book and the calculator and prepare to dazzle the family.

WORD FINDER

All you have to do is take away 2500 from the total. Nothing more, nothing less. Whatever the total, you always take away 2500. The new total contains all your information.

The last two digits show the word number counting in from the start of the line. The next two digits are the line number down from the top of the page. The remaining digits are the page number.

PLAY TO THE CROWD

If you want to add some drama to the trick, you could close your eyes in great concentration and hold the book to your forehead. It will add to the suspense even if no one believes you can do what you have said.

Finally, open the book to the page you have identified. Count down to the correct line. And count along to the correct word.

Ask the person who chose it to quietly confirm that it is the right word and then announce, modestly, what the word is.

If the family still don't believe you, repeat the trick with a different person, a different book and even a different calculator. It works every time if you follow the instructions.

Puzzle The Family With Riddles

WHO'S GOT THE QUICKEST BRAIN IN YOUR FAMILY?

Does Mum have the quickest brain, because she can do any number of things at the same time? Does Dad, because he thinks he knows more than anyone else? The point about a quick brain is that you don't need to know lots of information about lots of different things. It's the way you think – the way your brain works through a problem like a computer. That's what gives you a quick brain.

People have been pitting their wits against each other with riddles for thousands of years. So try out these top ten on the family and discover who can solve them quickest. (You'll find the answers on page 188.)

The first riddle is over 600 years old. It was set by Dr Claretus, a monk who lived in Bohemia and loved riddles.

* Like grass it is green, but it is not grass;
Like blood it is red, but it is not blood.
It is round and smooth like an egg.
What is it?

* It has towns but no houses;
It has forests, but no trees;
It has rivers, but no fish.
What is it?

* Something was here since the world was
First made, and just a month old.
What is it?

* What is it that a mother loves very dearly
But which can never welcome her when she comes home?

* The air alone gives birth to this.
It lives without a body.
It hears without ears.
It speaks without a mouth.
What is it?

* A man went for a walk.
It started to rain.
The man didn't have a hat.
He wasn't carrying an umbrella.
He kept on walking.
His clothes got wet.
His shoes got wet.
But his hair didn't get wet.
How come?

* A boy's grandfather is only five years older than the boy's father.
How come?

* What is too much for one, enough for two, but nothing at all for three?

* There was a green house.
Inside the green house there was a white house.
Inside the white house there was a red house.
Inside the red house there were a lot of little black beetles.
You are looking for fruit.
Which one?

* I am a poor iron knight,
I have no arms but always point right.
I have no feet but I must always go
And must stand on duty both day and night through.
If ever I rest, all will complain.
What am I?

SLICE A BANANA WITHOUT PEELING IT

Who says you can't slice a banana without peeling it? Just about everybody ... everybody that is who doesn't know this clever trick. So, see who is the first to work out how to do what looks like the impossible.

THE SECRET

The secret is to use a sewing needle. Push the needle into the banana at one of the 'seams'. Then wiggle the needle from side to side inside the banana, so that you cut across the fruit.

When you're sure that you've sliced right through, withdraw the needle, move it along the seam to the next place where you want to slice it and repeat the process. Carry on doing this until the banana is sliced into as many pieces as you want.

If you want to surprise your family, you should prepare the banana beforehand and then hide it in a fruit bowl without anyone seeing. From the outside your 'sliced' banana will look like any other banana. All you have to do is wait for the startled reaction when someone begins to peel it and slices of banana tumble out.

A WORD OF WARNING

One thing to watch for is that you don't prepare your trick banana too long before someone in the family 'discovers' it. If you secretly slice it too early, the banana will start to go brown where the needle has pierced it, and this will give the game away.

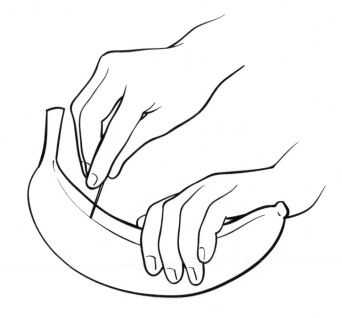

HOW TO SPEND £1 MILLION IN 24 HOURS

The choice is yours and what a choice it is! Try to imagine what you could buy in 24 hours if you had £1 million to spend. What would it be: designer clothes; a luxury car; a holiday of a lifetime; a trip into space; a second home? You could have all of these.

Each member of the family writes their own shopping list. The person who comes nearest to spending £1 million is the winner – and in this spending spree you can have more than one of any of the items listed. (If there is a tie, the person with the highest number of *different* items is the winner.)

* Helicopter: £600,000

* Sweet shop: £130,000

* Savings account: £100,000

* Rolls-Royce Phantom: £250,000

* Top of the range hi-fi equipment: £113,000

* Clothes shopping in a leading department store: £5,000

* Château in France: £350,000

* Home cinema: £34,000

* Ferrari Spider: £135,000

* Top of the range grand piano: £100,000

* Family holiday of a lifetime: £36,000

* Round-the-world cruise for two: £121,000

* Travel in space: £115,000 (per person)

* Five pairs of designer shoes: £4,000

* Flat in New York City: £270,000

How To Decide Who In The Family To Eat First

In old stories about sailors marooned on a desert island with nothing to eat, it's usually the cabin boy who gets eaten first. But this may not always be the best choice. Young people often have better eyesight than people who are older and a cabin boy with sharp eyes might spot a rescue ship that other people might not see.

Another important thing to consider is how much there is to eat on a cabin boy. They were usually scrawny and thin, and probably didn't provide a very good meal. Perhaps one of the others would be a better choice to pop into the pot first. It's not a decision you should rush into. Here are some things to discuss and consider.

FOOD FOR THOUGHT

* How useful are members of the family on the desert island? In other words, who does the least work? Maybe that person should be the first to be eaten? (Family slackers might want to think about this one – and then do something about it!)

* What about food supplies? Who eats the most at the moment? If that person joined the food supplies, perhaps everyone else would have more to eat for longer?

* Who would make the tastiest meal?

* Which member of the family would be the easiest to catch? You don't want to see your next meal disappearing into the distance because they run faster than anyone else.

* Which member of the family is the most expensive when you are at home? Cutting out the costs of this person could mean having more money to share among the rest of the family when you get back to civilization.

LIGHTING A CAMPFIRE WITHOUT MATCHES

Early humans made a fire without matches and modern humans (even modern fathers) can make fire, too, using the same primitive methods.

SAFETY FIRST WITH FIRE

It is essential to remember that early humans didn't have neighbours living right next door or farmers with valuable crops. So modern fire-makers must take precautions to prevent their fires getting out of control. Having a bucket of water or sand to put out the fire is a sensible idea. You should also make sure that there is nothing nearby that could catch light if your fire flares up, or sparks are blown from it by the wind. For this reason you shouldn't make fires in wooded areas where dried leaves and dead branches could catch light. If you decide to experiment in the garden, cut a piece of turf half a metre square from the lawn and put it to one side, grass side upwards. If you water this, the grass will survive and you can replace the turf to cover over your fire site when you have finished.

THE SECRET OF TINDER

Once your fire is alight you will need something to keep it burning. Dry branches are ideal fuel. Collect some and leave them out of the rain for a few weeks so they'll be ready for your fire-making experiment.

Before adding the branches, you will need tinder. This is the very fine, very dry material, which catches light first and is your fuel. Early humans used shredded bark, dry grass, dry moss or thin dry leaves. You could use the same. Make sure that you have enough to add to the fire once the first tinder is alight.

After the tinder is alight, you will need kindling: small dry sticks, no thicker than a pencil. These will help the fire get established before you start to add the fuel.

THE VITAL SPARK

Now for the fun part – though it will require patience. There are various ways that you can experiment with making fire. In every case you should try to ignite a small piece of tinder before adding more tinder and then the kindling.

∗ You can build up enough heat to light tinder by quickly twisting the end of a dry stick inside a hole in a piece of wood. Rub the stick between the palms of your hands, very fast. This creates friction. Friction creates heat. Heat creates a thin wisp of smoke. When you see that starting to appear, drop small pieces of tinder into the hole. Let these begin to smoulder, then add more tinder, blowing it gently to help it catch alight. When the tinder is burning, add some kindling and when that is burning as well, start to add the fuel, building the sticks into a pyramid over the fire.

∗ Instead of twisting a stick, you can try striking two sharp stones together. This will create sparks that can be directed onto tinder to set it alight.

∗ On bright, sunny days you can also try a method of making fire which early humans would not have used: this involves a magnifying glass. Hold the magnifying glass above some tinder and draw it upwards until the circle of sunlight shining through it is concentrated into a tiny point of bright light. Hold this steady over the same spot and a wisp of smoke will soon appear, which you can blow into a flame before adding tinder and fuel as above.

French Cricket For The Family

French cricket can be enjoyed in the garden, in the park, on the beach – anywhere where there is some open space. It doesn't require a lot of equipment either. A bat and ball are all you need – and you can play with any number of players, though between four and six are best.

GETTING STARTED

1 The ball should not be too hard or too bouncy – an old tennis ball is ideal.

2 The bat can be a small cricket bat (the most popular choice for French cricket), a rounders bat, a cricket stump or a tennis racket.

3 One player is the batsman, the others are fielders.

4 The object of the fielders is to get batsmen out by hitting their legs with the ball below the knee, or to catch the ball according to the rules opposite.

5 The object for the batsman is to protect his legs with the bat and to score one point for every ball hit.

6 The batsman with the highest number of points is the winner.

PLAYING FRENCH CRICKET

✳ Suppose Mum bats first.

✳ She stands with her legs together, holding the bat in front of her legs to protect them from the ball.

✳ Someone takes the ball and bowls it underarm (the ball is *always* bowled underarm in French cricket), trying to hit Mum on the legs below her knees.

✳ The other players stand in a circle round Mum, waiting to catch or stop the ball after she hits it.

✳ When Mum hits the ball, she can turn to face the person who stops it, because that person is the next bowler.

✳ But if she doesn't hit the ball, Mum is not allowed to move her feet. Because she isn't allowed to turn round to face the next bowler, she has to twist her body and try to protect her legs as best she can.

✳ The fielders have to bowl the ball from the place where they stop it.

✳ If they catch the ball, Mum is out and the next batsman has a go to try and score more points than Mum.

✳ You can also play a rule that Mum can be out if a fielder catches the ball with one hand after it has bounced once. This is known as 'one hand, one bounce'.

✳ After everyone has had a go at batting, the player with the highest number of points is 'Le Champion de la Famille'.

How To Sing A Round Together

Rounds are described as 'circles of sound', because rounds are songs that a group of people sing at different stages. As one part of the round is coming to an end, the other parts are still being sung, until the round finally comes full circle and stops. The fun of singing rounds is that different lines of the song are sung by different people at the same time.

Singing the same song together is enjoyable, but singing a round produces a lovely combination of sounds. You can buy books and CDs of rounds, but here is a very popular traditional round that is sung in many parts of the world. The words are in French, but they are easy to learn.

ROUND YOU GO

It's a good idea for everyone to sing through the song together to begin with, so that you all know the tune and understand how the words are pronounced. (Besides, it's a good opportunity for the family language experts to show off their knowledge of French.)

Frère Jacques, Frère Jacques,
Dormez-vous? Dormez-vous?
Sonnez les matines, sonnez les matines
Din dan don, din dan don.

In English this means:

Brother John, Brother John,
Are you sleeping, are you sleeping?
Morning bells are ringing, morning bells are ringing
Ding dang dong, ding dang dong.

TAKE IT AWAY IN PAIRS

If there are four people singing, why not start by singing in pairs – to practise how the round should be sung?

Ready? Off you go . . .

1 The first pair starts singing:

Frère Jacques, Frère Jacques,

2 As they are about to start the second line, the second pair begin with:

Frère Jacques, Frère Jacques,

3 As they are singing this, the first pair are singing:

> *Dormez-vous? Dormez-vous?*

4 Then the first pair move to line three and sing:

> *Sonnez les matines, sonnez les matines*

5 While the second pair sing:

> *Dormez-vous? Dormez-vous?*

6 The first pair reach the last line and sing:

> *Din dan don, din dan don.*

7 As the second pair are singing:

> *Sonnez les matines, sonnez les matines*

8 And the second pair end the round by singing the last line themselves:

> *Din dan don, din dan don.*

SOLO TURNS

Once you know the tune and have practised the round in pairs, you will be ready to sing it by yourselves, with each person starting a line as the person before starts the next line.

This means that the last person to sing will start singing the first line (*Frère Jacques, Frère Jacques*) when the first singer is starting the last line of the round (*Din dan don, din dan don*). The other two singers are each singing the lines in between.

But you don't have to stop when the first singer reaches the end of the last line. They can go back to the beginning and start the round all over again, leading the other singers through it line by line as many times as you like.

How To Produce Money Magically From Nowhere

Everyone would like to be able to produce money with a click of their fingers and if you practise this magical masterpiece you'll be able to do just that!

THE TRICK

You show your audience your empty hands. You pull up your sleeves to show that there is nothing hidden. Then you click your fingers and produce a neatly folded note – magic money masterfully manifested.

THE TECHNIQUE

1. You prepare the trick by folding the note and concealing it in the folds of your jacket sleeves (or any other long-sleeved garment you are wearing).

2. It won't fall out of where it's hidden, because you hold your hands upwards when showing people that your hands are empty.

3. Then, when you pull up your sleeves, you extract the note with your right hand as you are pulling up your left sleeve.

4. The note is hidden in the palm of your right hand.

5. You click the fingers of both hands, rub the palms together and produce the note.

6. Unfold it casually and hold it up so that everyone can admire your skill.

BE A BUTLER FOR A DAY

These days only the richest and poshest families employ butlers to look after them – but why should your family be left out? Since butlers are usually men, why not let the men in the family each have a go at working as butlers, taking care of the rest of the family for a day?

WHAT THE BUTLER WORE

Butlers are always very smartly dressed. These days they usually wear a black jacket, white shirt and black tie, and the kind of striped grey trousers that men wear at weddings. They wear black shoes, polished to a high shine. This is the uniform a butler wears when he is serving the family. When he is working in the butler's pantry, he takes off his jacket and wears an apron to keep his clothes clean.

THE WORKING MORNING

1 The butler needs to get up early in the morning to prepare breakfast, lay the breakfast table and be ready to serve tea or coffee to the family when they come down to eat. Families help themselves to what they want to eat for breakfast.

2 In many households, the butler irons the morning newspaper for his employer, to remove any creases.

3 Sometimes the butler also acts as his master's man-servant and lays out the clothes his master will wear.

4 After breakfast, the butler cleans away the plates, dishes, knives, forks and food and takes these to the kitchen to be washed and put away.

5 For the rest of the morning he has to listen for the telephone ringing or knocks at the door, while he goes about his other duties. If the phone rings, the butler answers, saying something like 'This is Mrs Johnson's residence. Johnson the butler speaking. How can I help you?' He then either lets them know that they have a telephone call or, if they are out, he takes a message.

6 If someone calls at the house, the butler (wearing his jacket, not his apron) answers the doorbell, opening the door and saying something like, 'Good morning sir/madam. How can I help you?'

7 If the visitor is making a delivery, the butler could send them to the 'tradesman's entrance' (the back door), where he will take the delivery himself.

8 If the visitor has come to see a member of the family, the butler will invite them to step inside, before leading them to the room where the family member can be found. He will knock gently at the door and when told to enter, will open the door announcing 'Mrs Moreton to see you, Mrs Johnson'.

9 For the rest of the morning the butler will be busy checking that the rooms in the house are properly heated, that fresh flowers are put in every room and that any post is delivered to the member of the family it is addressed to.

LUNCH IS SERVED

1 Lunch is served at 1.00 pm, which means that the table must be correctly laid and the butler must be standing by to serve the family as soon as he has announced that lunch is ready.

2 Soup will be the first course and he carries a large bowl of soup to each person at the table.

3 The butler will also be responsible for serving wine, water and any other drinks with the meal, refilling glasses when they are empty.

4 He offers second helpings and then clears away the soup bowls ready for the main course.

5 If roast meat is being served, the butler will carve this. Otherwise he will take portions of the main course to everyone at the table and then offer two or three different vegetables.

6 When the main course is finished and cleared away, the butler will serve the dessert course.

7 This could be followed by a cheese course.

8 When everyone has finished, the butler will ask the lady of the house where she would like him to serve coffee. He then serves coffee in the drawing room, in the garden, or wherever else she suggests.

AFTERNOON DUTIES

1 When the family has finished lunch and left to spend the afternoon doing whatever they want, the butler clears away. He then lays the dining table for dinner and returns to the butler's pantry to carry on with his duties.

2 These might include: cleaning and polishing the silver; cleaning and checking the glassware; or bringing wine and other drinks from the cellar and preparing them for dinner.

3 At tea-time (between 4.00 and 4.30 pm) the butler will serve tea to the family, having asked the lady of the house where she would prefer to take tea.

4 In the early evening, before dinner is served, he will offer to serve drinks to the family. In some modern households the butler also switches on the television and finds a favourite programme for the family to watch.

DINNER IS SERVED

1 The last meal of the day is dinner, to which the family may have invited guests. When they arrive, the butler greets them, takes their coats and hats and leads them to where the family are gathered, in order to announce their arrival.

2 When dinner is ready, the butler will make an announcement and will then serve the meal in the same way as lunch.

3 After dessert, the ladies will probably leave the dining room to take coffee in the drawing room. The butler will then serve port to the gentlemen still sitting at the table, before leaving them.

AND SO TO BED

1 Before leaving the family to enjoy their evening, the butler will need to check that they have everything they need and that the fires or heating are in order.

2 He then waits in his pantry in case the family call for him.

3 When it is time for the guests to leave, he will give them their coats and hats and possibly show them to their cars under an umbrella if it is raining.

4 Finally he will check that his employers have everything they need for the night, before locking the house, switching off all electrical equipment and turning off the lights.

5 Then – and only then – can the butler get ready for bed himself.

SQUARE CUTS

Here are two tests to see who in the family has the quickest mind and is snappiest with scissors. Keep this page covered until everyone has what they need: paper, pencil, ruler, eraser and a pair of scissors. Then reveal the page, so that everyone can see it.

CHALLENGE 1

1 Get everyone to copy the cross shown below.

2 See who is first to work out a way of dividing it into four pieces, using just *two* straight cuts, so that the pieces can be put together to form a perfect square!

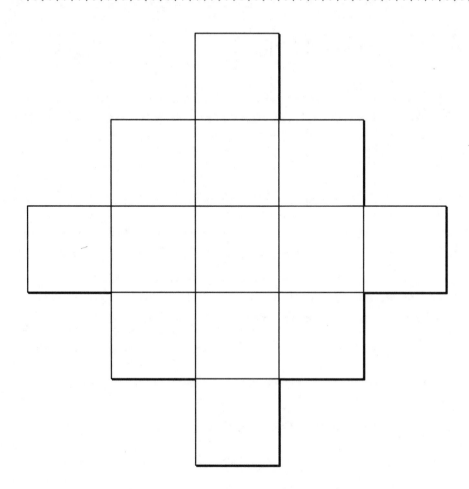

CHALLENGE 2

❶ Now get everyone to copy the diagram shown here.

❷ This time, see who is first to crack dividing it into four pieces, identical in size and shape, so that the pieces can be put together to form a perfect square.

The answers to both challenges are on page 189.

THE THREE-CUP TRICK

This is a very old fairground trick that has been fooling audiences for many years. It's simple to perform, but it still baffles people who don't know how it works. So, who better to try it on than the rest of the family? Let them each have a turn to see if they can work out how to solve it.

THREE CUPS – THREE MOVES

Place three identical cups in a row on a table – paper cups would be perfect. The two end cups need to be facing downward and the middle one facing upward.

Now tell the person whose go it is that he or she has three moves to make all three cups end up in the same position – *facing upward*. In each move, the person handling the cups can reverse the direction of any *two* cups, so that they face up or down.

✳ To show what you mean, you move the cups first. Start with them like this:

✳ Now move cups A and B, so that the three look like this:

✱ Next move cups A and C, so that the three look like this:

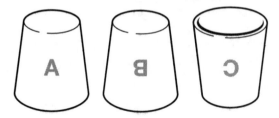

✱ Finally, move cups A and B. Hey presto! All three are facing upwards. It couldn't be simpler.

SETTING UP THE CON

✱ Now comes the real con! To ensure Dad looks decidedly dumb you need to arrange them to look like this:

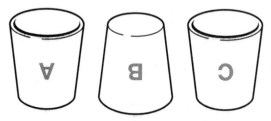

Yes – you've got it. The cups are *not* in the same order they were in when you demonstrated the trick. Check for yourself. The two end cups are facing upward and the middle one is facing downward. Because you've changed their starting positions, the best anyone can achieve is to have all three cups facing *downward* – the opposite to what you asked for and what you demonstrated.

You'll be surprised how long it takes for people to spot how you've tricked them.

Magic Squares

In these three magic squares each of the nine digits appears only once. Each magic square works in a similar way to other magic squares, with every line of numbers having the same total.

However, in these magic squares you reach the total in an unusual way. Instead of adding all three numbers in a line to reach the common answer, you add two and subtract the third. And in each row, column and diagonal of all three squares the common answer is five.

Here's an example to get you started: in the top row of the first magic square $2 + 4 = 6$ and $6 - 1 = 5$.

Now see who is first in the family to work out how the other answers to each row, column and diagonal are reached.

2	1	4
3	5	7
6	9	8

8	1	4
3	5	7
6	9	2

2	1	6
3	5	7
4	9	8

How To Have Fun In The Sun

More effective than the old 'towel on the sunbed' ploy, here are some tips and tricks guaranteed to earn your family an excellent space on a previously packed beach. Watch as people edge away...

* Sit down to very elaborate picnics with proper cutlery, maybe a candlestick or two and a wine cooler, and eat your way slowly through several courses.

* Get Dad to start singing, something obscure and operatic is ideal, then gradually all join in until you reach a rousing climax.

* Find large pieces of stinking seaweed and drag them to form a circle around the area of sand you are sitting on.

* Make sure that everyone in the family goes into the sea about 15 minutes after lunch and stays waist-deep in the water for 10 minutes. Then watch to see how many people swim in that spot afterwards.

* Loudly refuse to eat ice cream being sold on the beach, expressing grave health concerns – especially if everyone around you is eating it.

* Pretend to have a terrible family row – everyone near you will want to listen in, but will feel guilty about doing so.

* Start scratching yourselves all over and slap at the sand, as if you are swatting biting insects.

* Don't settle – keep fidgeting with everything: your sunbeds, your parasol, your clothes, your shoes, your picnic, everything you have brought with you.

How To Make And Use Tangrams

The tangram is an ancient form of puzzle from China. A tangram set consists of seven pieces, formed by dissecting a square as shown in this diagram. Any material can be used, provided that it is reasonably stiff and can be cut accurately into the shapes below: card is ideal.

The object of a tangram puzzle is to arrange the seven pieces to form a specific shape. All the pieces must be used and no piece may overlap another.

Imagine the figures below are people or pets in your family. See if you can arrange the seven tangram pieces to make ...

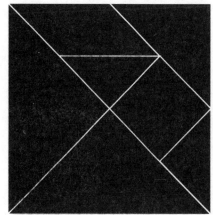

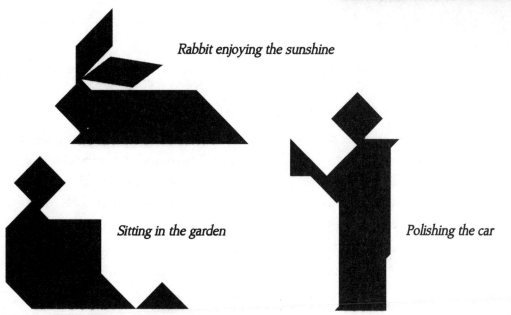

Rabbit enjoying the sunshine

Sitting in the garden

Polishing the car

MAKE A FAMILY PHOTO COLLAGE

Is yours one of those families with loads of photographs no one ever looks at? You know what happens – the pictures are taken, everyone gathers round to look at them the first time, then they are put away and forgotten about.

Wouldn't it be great to have a special display where you could have all sorts of family photographs – holiday snaps, birthday pictures, days out, dressing-up, school sports, special events – a big selection all together for everyone to enjoy for a while? After a few months, you could change the pictures and set up a new display.

This kind of mixed display is known as a collage. They're fun to make and they'll remind your family of things you've done together which you may have forgotten about.

COLLAGE CREATION

✳ The best way to create a collage is to use a large picture mount with a solid back and a sheet of glass that is clipped on to it. You can buy these in art shops and some DIY stores.

✳ If you want to be able to change pictures after a while, use colour copies of photographs and a removable glue that will hold them in place, but will still let you lift them off the backing when you want to.

✳ Don't just stick down pictures in any old fashion. Try to put them together in amusing ways. You might have a picture of Mum laughing her head off. This would look great alongside a picture of someone else in the family accidentally falling into a pool of water. You could even put Mum's head onto the body of someone falling into a pool.

✳ Perhaps there's a picture of Dad looking puzzled and confused. This could look very funny beside a picture of him trying to mend the lawn mower, with parts of the machine spread on the ground. You get the idea.

* Pictures of the kids when they were small, looking up at something, could go beside pictures of them when they are older looking down at something.

* Don't be afraid to cut around people to get them out of one picture and put them into another (make sure everyone is happy for you to cut up the picture first, though).

* Use your imagination, get everyone to work on the collage together and you can have a hilarious time reliving past glories, embarrassments and disasters.

HOW TO BE THE ROYAL FAMILY

Don't be mistaken – being the royal family requires a lot of hard work and you don't get much privacy. However, if you still like the idea of convincing the neighbours you're the nation's number one family, here are some ideas to help you make a start.

* The obvious place to start is adding titles to your names. Dad should put King in front of his first name. Mum should put Queen in front of hers. The rest of the family can use either Prince or Princess.

* Change the name of your house. You can't really call a royal residence 'Palace No. 4, Lake View Crescent'. It's probably better to go for something bolder, such as: 'Luton Palace', or 'Oldham Castle'.

* Order new writing paper with this address and a crown above it. (Order new envelopes with a crown stamped on the back flap – that looks very classy.)

* Buy a few Corgis and perhaps a couple of black Labradors.

* Always wear your best clothes when you are out and about.

* Arrange for large, highly polished, black cars to collect you from your house. Ask the driver to drive slowly through busy streets, so that you can move your hand just a little as you wave and smile at people looking at you.

* Arrange for other members of the family to telephone hotels where you are staying, or the houses of friends you are visiting. When people answer the calls they'll be able to give you messages like: 'The prime minister apologises for interrupting you, Your Majesty, but he needs to speak to you urgently on a secure line.'

* When people ask where you are going on holiday, tell them 'Scotland, as usual.' And for Christmas? 'At Windsor, with the family. Then to Norfolk, as we do every year.'

MAKE A BOTTLE GARDEN

Bottle gardens are clean and tidy – and require almost no attention once they are made. You can buy the things you need to make one from a garden centre and make it on a table at home.

GARDEN PLANNER

To make a bottle garden you will need: a large glass bottle with a lid; small pebbles; small pieces of charcoal; damp soil; several small plants; a large spoon or trowel.

GARDEN MAKER

1. Remove the lid from the glass jar and lay it on its side.

2. Place a layer of pebbles on the bottom of the jar.

3. On top of this spread a layer of charcoal.

4. Spread a layer of damp soil over the charcoal.

5. Use the spoon or trowel to make shallow holes in the soil.

6. Insert a few small plants (ferns, ivy and African violets are popular choices).

7. Cover the roots with soil and sprinkle water over the plants.

8. Replace the lid on the bottle, making sure that it fits tightly.

9. Put the bottle in a warm, light place.

10. Watch the plants continue to grow healthily as the water is recycled inside the glass jar.

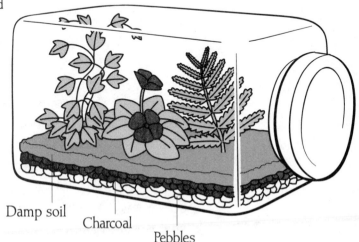

Damp soil   Charcoal   Pebbles

Escape From A Charging Elephant

Seeing animals in the wild is a thrilling experience, but sometimes the animals can come too close for comfort. Before the family jumps in a jeep and sets off on a safari, it's a good idea to know how to escape an elephant in a mood.

SAFETY FIRST

Elephants may look slow and slightly dozy sometimes, but an elephant can run faster than a human when it wants to. The best way of staying safe is not to put yourselves in danger. That's easy to say, but in the excitement of a 'holiday of a lifetime' it's also easy to forget.

You can picture the scene. Dad's got a new camera and wants to get the best pictures because this might be the only elephant the family sees. He gets out of the vehicle and moves closer to the elephant. Mum tells him to be careful, but she can see he isn't listening. Flash goes the anti red-eye button, causing the elephant to look up self-consciously. It sees a badly dressed guy with a camera walking towards it. Out go the elephant's ears and it starts moving towards Dad – slowly at first then gathering speed. How should Dad react?

THINGS DAD SHOULD NOT DO

✳ Take a live mouse from his pocket and dangle it in front of the elephant. (Elephants are only frightened of mice in stories.)

✳ Run towards the elephant shaking his fist.

✳ Throw rocks at the elephant.

✳ Lie down and pretend to be dead. (Elephants aren't stupid.)

THINGS DAD COULD DO

✳ Get Mum to drive the jeep towards him, so that he can jump into the passenger seat and the family can speed away.

✳ Run to a nearby tree and climb into it. Dad will have to stay in the tree until the elephant gives up and goes away. Then Mum can collect him in the jeep.

✳ Run away from the elephant towards bushes or rocks, *but* run in sharp zig-zags. The elephant is much heavier than Dad and can't change direction as easily or as quickly as he can.

✳ Jump into a river and swim underwater downstream until he finds somewhere to hide in the reeds on the riverbank.

CONNECT THESE NINE DOTS WITH FOUR LINES

Which family member can work out a way of drawing four straight lines through these nine dots without lifting the pen or pencil from the paper?

All you need is a pen or pencil to draw with and a piece of paper for each person. Copy the square of dots as shown and then start experimenting. Remember, though, pens or pencils have to stay on the paper; they can't be lifted after a line has been drawn. (You'll find the answer on page 189.)

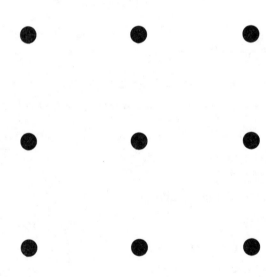

How To Play Horseshoe

Horseshoe is a perfect game to play on the aeroplane on your way to a holiday, or on the beach once you've arrived. It needs the minimum of equipment and it's played all over the world.

HOW TO PLAY

* Two players start with two counters or coins placed on a simple board, which can be drawn on a piece of paper or marked in the sand.

* If you use coins, play with one pair heads up, the other tails up.

* The counters or coins are placed in the positions shown on the right to start the game.

* The first player starts by moving one of his or her counters along a line to the empty point in the centre.

* The second player moves one of his or her counters along a line to the new vacant position.

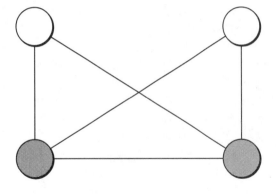

* Play continues alternately, each player moving one of his or her counters along a line to a vacant point.

* The aim of the game is to block an opponent, so that neither of his or her counters can be moved.

* In this example, the player with the white counters can move into a winning position.

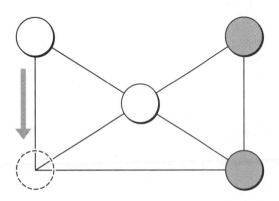

How To Be The Best Recycler In The Family

How many families look inside their dustbins to see what has been thrown out for the bin men to take away? If more did, they might see that lots of things – glass bottles, plastic bottles, aluminium cans, cereal boxes, newspapers, magazines, torch batteries, raw vegetables, dead flowers – have been thrown away that could be recycled.

Once a household gets hooked on recycling, it can become quite competitive. Check on how much *less* your family is putting out for the bin men than you used to – that shows how much *more* is being recycled. Run a competition between yourselves, to see who is the best recycler at home.

GOING GREEN

* Start by putting up a wall chart beside the back door leading to where the dustbin is kept. Keep a pen or pencil nearby.

* Along the top of the chart, list all the things used at home that can be recycled.

* Down the side mark wide bands for each member of the family, so that every time that person recycles something in the list along the top, they can put a mark below it next to their name.

This way, everyone can see who is recycling what. The more marks a person has, the better they are doing.

WHERE TO RECYCLE

Someone in the family has to do the research to find what can be recycled, where and when in your neighbourhood. That can take some time and careful planning. So there's another challenge. Who in the family can find the most recycling places within five miles of home? That should keep everyone busy.

There are recycling bins for cans, bottles and paper in supermarket car parks, public car parks and lots of other places – finding one shouldn't be a problem. Councils also have special centres that recycle everything from TVs and computers, to old car batteries and fridges. In centres like these you will find somewhere to recycle most things that you want to get rid of.

Very little needs to be thrown away. Shoes and clothes that the family no longer need can be collected by charities in special bins and given to people who are really pleased to receive them. The same goes for furniture, computers and kitchen appliances that a family may be changing. These can be collected and given to people who need them – and this counts as recycling.

A LOT OF ROT

There is a lot of kitchen waste that you can recycle at home instead of throwing in the bin. Fruit and vegetable leaves, peelings and other parts that aren't going to be eaten can be collected and used to make compost to help plants grow and improve soil in the family garden. (Find out about composting on page 38.)

How To Hold Someone Down On A Chair With Just Your Little Finger

Even the smallest member of the family will be able to keep the biggest pinned down on a chair using just a little finger. It sounds incredible, but it can be done if it's done the right way.

HEAD UP

1 The person on the chair must sit with their head back and their chin up.

2 The person holding them down places a little finger against their forehead and asks them to get up.

3 No cheating is allowed – for example, they mustn't try to wriggle out sideways, or try to knock the little finger away.

4 If they carry out these instructions correctly, the person in the chair is at the mercy of the one holding them down and they certainly won't be able to stand up.

5 The reason for this is that the sitter's head has to move forwards slightly before they can stand up and it's this forward movement that can be stopped quite easily, even by a little finger.

WIN 'PICK UP THE LAST PENNY' EVERY TIME

There aren't many games people can be sure of winning every time they play, but this game is one of them – so long as the winning player is polite enough to let the other player have the first go.

AFTER YOU

This is what happens.

1 One player challenges the other that they will pick up the last penny from 20 spread on a table.

2 The same player also allows the other player to have the first go – after all it is only polite. (*Actually making the other player go first is the secret of winning the game.*)

3 Each player is allowed to pick up one, two or three coins in turn – with the winner being the one to pick up the last coin.

4 The secret is being able to count to four – nothing else!

5 However many coins the first player first picks up (one, two or three), their opponent must make the total of both their goes add up to four.

6 So, if the player who goes first picks up two coins, the second player needs to pick up two coins as well (2 + 2 = 4).

7 This means that the remaining coins will always be divisible by four, since 20 is divisible by four in the first place.

8 By the first player's fifth go, there will only be four coins left.

9 Since the highest number of coins that can be picked up in a go is three, the second player wins whatever happens.

10 In fact – making sure the first player goes first guarantees that the second player will pick up the last penny and win the game, so long as they know the secret.

Stop Runaway Horses

Riding is an enjoyable way for the family to spend time together and get out into the countryside, but, should anything go wrong, what started out as a gentle hack through the woods and fields can become a terrifying experience.

What happens, for example, if the horse you're riding is spooked by something and breaks into a gallop so suddenly that you lose hold of the reins? How do you stop it? What can you do if there is a busy road ahead and your horse is galloping flat out towards it?

BLIND SPOT

✱ Having lost your reins you won't be able to pull on them to stop the horse in the usual way.

✱ Grip the saddle with your knees so that you can carefully take off your jacket or pullover.

✱ Hold one cuff in each hand.

✱ Lean forward and swing the garment you are holding over the horse's head.

✱ Pull down on the sleeves, so that the pullover or jacket covers the horse's eyes.

✱ Cling on with your knees and wait for the horse to slow down. Once it can no longer see where it is going the horse will stop galloping, allowing you to regain control and bring it to a halt before you reach the dangerous road.

Prepare A Spooky Hallowe'en Supper

Hallowe'en is the perfect night for a spooky supper. The room can be lit by flickering candlelight and scary pumpkin masks with nightlights glowing inside them. The table can be laid with a blood-red tablecloth and the menu can have all kinds of ghastly, ghostly dishes from Ghoulish Gruel with Eye Balls (which is actually beef stew with dumplings) to Bubbling Maggots Bake (which is macaroni cheese).

Here are half-a-dozen other dishes for a meal to remember:

* Witches' Brew – Soup made from carrots or pumpkins, with tinned tomatoes added to give a redder colour and a lumpy texture.

* Baked Fingers – Thin cooked sausages, with a plain blanched almond pressed into one end. Serve in a napkin-lined basket, with the fingers poking over the side to look even more scary.

* Floating Corpse Hand – A cool drink with a difference. Fill a clean rubber glove with any green-coloured soft drink (lime cordial, for example). Fasten the end and pop it in the freezer. When it's frozen, take it out and dip it quickly in warm water to make it easier to remove the glove. Float the icy hand in a bowl with orange squash or a diluted blackcurrant drink.

* Witches' Hair and Cats' Eyeballs – Finely shredded carrots and cabbage (to make the hair) and green grapes for the eyeballs. Serve in a bowl and add French dressing for drop of slime.

* Zombie Oozings – Baked jacket potatoes, slit open with some of the potato scooped out to look as though it's oozing out on its own. Garnish with tomato ketchup (for blood) and mustard (for whatever else your imagination conjures up).

MAKE AND USE FAMILY CODE MACHINES

You don't need to have a lot of complicated equipment to send and read secret messages. Simple code machines like the one described here can be made by anyone, anywhere. As long as the person receiving the message has the same kind of machine, they will be able to read the message even though it won't make any sense at all to anyone else.

Get everyone in the family to make a code machine following these instructions, so that you can send secret messages to each other by email, text, letter, postcard – even by pigeon if you want to be different!

BOXING CLEVER

1 Draw 52 boxes measuring 5mm x 10mm side by side on a slip of paper or card.

2 Write out the alphabet, placing one letter in each box, starting with A on the far left of the strip. B goes in the next box along and so on, moving box-by-box to the right.

3 When you reach Z continue with the alphabet a second time until you finish with Z again on the far right of the strip.

4 Now prepare a second strip with boxes the same size, but this time you only need to draw 26 boxes.

5 Write out the alphabet again in the shorter strip, one letter per box, again moving from left to right. When both strips are complete, you'll have your code machine.

`A B C D E F G H I J K L M N O P Q R S T U V W X Y Z`

`A B C D E F G H I J K L M N O P Q R S T U V W X Y Z A B C D E F G H I J K L M N O P Q R S T U V W X Y Z`

CODING/DECODING

1 To make a code, position the short strip above the long strip, so that the boxes line up with the ones below. Suppose the A in the short strip is directly above the J in the long strip. When you write your message you must use the letter J every time you would normally use the letter A. In the same way, B would be written in code using K and C would be coded as L.

2 Make sure that the person to whom you are sending the message knows which code you are using. The example shown on page 134 uses Code J so the first letter of your message should be a circled J so that the recipient knows how to set up their code machine correctly in order to start decoding it.

3 Imagine that the first word of the message you want to send is CANCEL. In Code J that would be written as Ⓙ LJWLNU.

4 When the message is received, the recipient places the short strip in the correct position and decodes it using the coded letters from the longer strip.

MAKE MUM AN EGYPTIAN MUMMY

The ancient Egyptians used to preserve the bodies of important people to make sure their souls would have something to live in in the afterlife. And who is more important to preserve than a parent?

To carry out the following experiment requires a degree of consent on the part of the 'victim'. If it's Mum's turn to become that other kind of mummy, tell her not to complain too much, because the rest of the family are going to take special care of her and she won't need to lift a finger – in fact she won't be able to lift a finger (or anything else for that matter).

WASH AND WRAP

So, the first thing to do with the family mummy is to ask her to have a good wash. In ancient Egypt spiced palm wine was used, but a nice-smelling bath gel would do just as well. Make sure the mummy dries herself well before the next stage begins – wrapping the body in metres of strips of material.

It's probably best if Mum puts on a swimsuit before the rest of the family get to work on her. When she's ready, she stands somewhere where Dad and the kids can move easily round her while they work. Make sure she is comfortable – because the afterlife lasts a very long time!

Ancient Egyptian mummies had their brains removed (pulled out through their noses). The organs (the lungs, liver, stomach and intestines) were removed as well, with only the heart being left in place. With Mum, though, it's probably best to leave everything inside her where it belongs.

TEAM WORK WITH TISSUE

Egyptian mummies were wrapped in 20 layers of linen strips. Hundreds of metres of material were used and the wrapping lasted for many days. Today's mummy will have to be wrapped rather more quickly than that and since strips of linen aren't easy to find, use rolls of bathroom tissue instead. This is more delicate than Egyptian linen and tears quite easily, so pass it round the mummy's body very carefully – handing it backwards and forwards as you wind it round and round the mummy.

If you start at the mummy's head, the wrappers need to leave the eyes, nose and mouth uncovered. You continue wrapping the body down the arms, down the body and down both legs to the ankles and feet. As you wrap, you can slip little charms, jewels and precious metals under the 'bandages' to supply the mummy with valuables in the afterlife. Prayers and magic words written on pieces of paper can be included in the wrapping as well – these help protect the mummy in the afterlife.

TOMB WORK

Once an Egyptian mummy was ready, it was placed in a beautifully decorated coffin and placed in a tomb. That's probably going a bit far with the family mummy. A few photographs for the family album will be a good enough record for the afterlife. Mum might choose to lie back and enjoy some peace and quiet before she is unwrapped and returned to the land of the living.

PLAY STEPPING STONES

This is a game that links words and requires no equipment except for imagination and a quick mind.

HOW TO PLAY

Each player is given five themes by the other players. For example, they might ask the player whose turn it is to get from Music to Astronomy by way of Cookery, Money and Cars. Now the player has to think up nine statements or phrases and use these as 'stepping stones' to move from the subject of Music to the subject of Astronomy. The other players in the

family act as umpires, checking that the stepping stones are reached in the correct order and that none of the connections between them are too far-fetched.

FOR EXAMPLE

Here's one way in which a player could get from Music to Astronomy, using words and ideas associated with Cookery, Money and Cars in that order:

1. A note can be flat or sharp. (Music)
2. Knives used in kitchens should always be sharp. (Cookery)
3. Knives are used for cutting.
4. When shops have sales, they cut their prices. (Money)
5. When the sales are on we can *afford* to buy more.
6. Mum and Dad's first car was a Ford. (Cars)
7. But what they'd really like is a Rolls.
8. The Rolling Stones are rock stars.
9. Stars are studied by astronomers. (Astronomy)

PLAY CHARADES

Charades is a great game that you can play at any family gathering. You can play in teams, or you can play individually. No equipment is needed – so Dad can't get out of playing because 'it will take too long to get organised'. Mum can show off her acting skills and everyone can have fun coming up with entertaining ideas to baffle the rest of the family.

THE SOUND OF SILENCE

Charades is a *miming* game. Players take it in turn to mime the titles of books, films, songs, and TV and radio programmes and the rest of the group try to guess what they are miming.

1 Each performance begins with the audience being informed how many words there are in the title. Remember this is a miming game, so the person performing cannot say a word.

If the title they have to guess is *The Lord of the Rings* for example, the player performing the mime would hold up five fingers to show that the audience have to identify five words from the mimes.

It's the title of a book.

It's the title of a film.

It's the title of a song.

It's the title of a TV show.

It's a short word.

2 Next, the miming player indicates whether the title applies to a book, a film, a song, or a TV or radio show, by using one or more of the hand gestures shown here (*The Lord of the Rings*, for example, is a book and a film).

3 Then they hold up one finger to show that they are about to mime the first word.

The is a small word and, again using hand gestures, the miming player indicates that the word the audience is looking for is short. When someone correctly calls out 'The', the player miming the title nods and gives a thumbs-up to indicate that *The* is correct.

4 Now they hold up two fingers, to indicate that the second word is about to be mimed. This time the mime depicts the word *Lord*.

5 The game continues like this, word by word, until someone in the audience suddenly sees the connection and calls out *The Lord of the Rings*. Then the miming player gives another thumbs-up sign and hands over to let someone else have a go.

6 Other clues players can give their audience include cupping an ear to indicate the word they are acting out *rhymes* with the word in the title, and holding fingers against their forearm to show the number of syllables a word contains.

How To Make This Uneven Carpet Square With Just Three Cuts

Imagine that this shape represents an unevenly cut carpet – the kind of thing that sometimes happens when Dad decides to save money on hiring a professional and has a go at fitting things himself. Now imagine that each member of the family has the job of sorting out Dad's little accident.

Mum decides that the neatest solution is to make the carpet square. The snag is that it can only be cut into *four* pieces. It's time for head scratching and puzzled brows. Who will be the first to find a way of doing this?

THE SET-UP

1 Ask everyone to copy this diagram.

2 Give each person a pair of scissors, or perhaps a ruler and pencil to begin with.

3 Set the clock and time how long it takes for the solution to be found.

The winner gets out of washing-up after the next meal. The answer is on page 190.

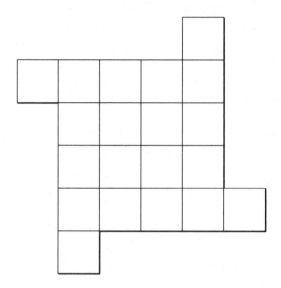

MULTIPLY IN DOUBLE-QUICK TIME

Announce to the family that you can multiply together any two numbers between 10 and 20 in your head. Enjoy the look of sheer disbelief on their faces when they check your mathematical prowess with a calculator and find out your multiplication skills are flawless.

METHOD

There's a cunning way of doing awkward sums like this in your head in a fraction of the time it normally takes.

1. Add the first number to the second digit of the second number.

2. Multiply by 10.

3. Now multiply the second digits of both numbers.

4. Finally, add together the two answers and you will have the answer to what looked like a difficult piece of multiplication.

EXAMPLES

* 13 x 19 = ?!
* 13 + 9 = 22
* 22 x 10 = 220
* 3 x 9 = 27
* Add 220 + 27 = 247
* 13 x 19 = 247

* 18 x 17 = ?!
* 18 + 7 = 25
* 25 x 10 = 250
* 8 x 7 = 56
* Add 250 + 56 = 306
* 13 x 19 = 306

Find Which Direction Is South When You're Lost

OK – who forgot to bring the compass? It's never a good idea to presume that the family member who was entrusted with the job of map-reading actually knows where the family is. You can tell by the slightly confused look on their face that nothing on the ground seems to match the map.

Don't panic, though. It's a sunny day and you've got a wristwatch with hands and a traditional clock-face. You may not realise it, but that means you've also got a simple form of compass! Follow these instructions and you'll soon find out where you are.

FROM CLOCK TO COMPASS

1. Take off the watch and hold it in the palm of your hand.

2. If you're in the northern hemisphere, turn the watch so that the hour hand is pointing towards the sun.

3. Look at the watch-face and note the direction in which 12 o'clock is pointing.

4. If you're in the southern hemisphere, turn the watch-face so that 12 o'clock is pointing towards the sun.

5. Look at the watch-face and note the direction in which the hour hand is pointing.

6. In both hemispheres, divide the angle between the two points you have noted in half (bisect it, in other words).

7. That bisecting line will point due south in the northern hemisphere and due north in the southern hemisphere.

8. Now turn the map so that it is pointing north–south and start correctly identifying features you can see.

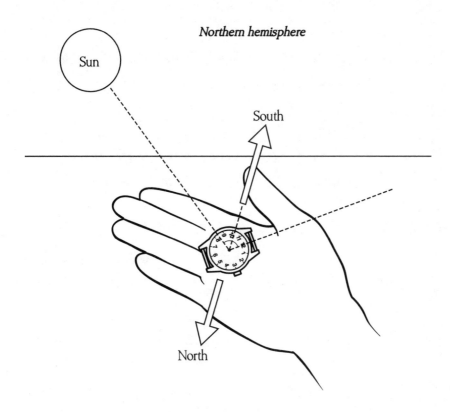

Oops – who forgot to bring the compass *and* forgot to bring a watch? Some families don't make life easy for themselves. Never mind, the sun is still shining and it's still morning, so you can find out where south is, but you'll need to be patient; it may take a few hours.

SUNDIAL COMPASS

1 Find a straight stick and put it in the ground in a place where you can mark its shadow.

2 Try to position the stick as vertically as you can. You can check this by making a simple plumb line with a piece of string and weight. You haven't got any string? OK, use a thread from your clothes with a button tied at the end to act as a weight.

3 Mark the end of the shadow cast by the stick.

4 Wait approximately half an hour and mark the end of the shadow again.

5 Keep doing this until you have made several marks (that's why you need to be patient).

6 The mark nearest the stick will represent the shortest shadow, which is cast at midday, when the sun is highest in the sky and pointing due south.

7 Pick a point in the distance along the line between the stick and the shortest shadow.

8 That point is south of where you are.

9 Now you can turn the map, like you did before, and find which way you should be travelling.

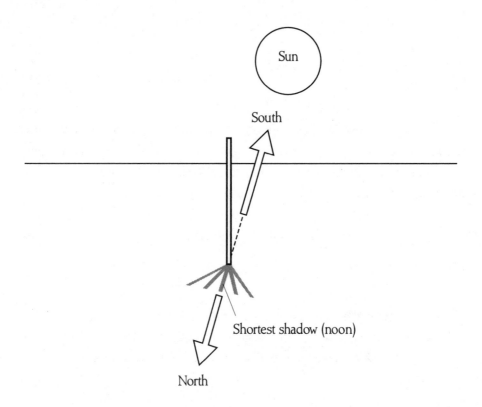

Sun

South

Shortest shadow (noon)

North

HOW TO BE THE GRINCH AT CHRISTMAS

Are there times when you get the feeling that the only person who had the right idea about the 'festive season' was 'The Grinch Who Stole Christmas'? Do you feel grumpy at the thought of goodwill to all men? Do you even make Scrooge seem generous?

Here are some suggestions on how to wreck your family Christmas. But you wouldn't ... would you?

GRINCH TIPS

* Return 'round-robin' Christmas letters to the senders enclosing a note saying something like, 'Someone is distributing this and using your name. I thought you should know.'

* Turn up the television volume when carol singers arrive and turn off the lights until they go away.

* On Christmas Eve send the television away for 'its annual service'.

* Fill children's stockings with 'useful presents' – revision cards for school exams, that kind of thing.

* Try to find the present you were given last year and give it back to the person who gave it to you.

* Buy crackers without any little gifts inside.

* Replace the usual riddles and jokes with miserable reflections on how hard life can be.

* Glue together paper hats, so that they tear when people try to open them.

* Duplicate presents and lose the receipts, so that they can't be returned or exchanged. If they happen to be things you want yourself, no problem. Just offer to take them back.

How To Convince Mum She Is Invisible

Does Mum ever complain she is taken for granted at home and might as well be invisible? It would be mean to convince her it's true, wouldn't it? Here's how:

✳ When 'invisible' Mum appears and says hi, everyone should look around to see where she is.

✳ When 'invisible' Mum asks what's going on, pretend you think that she is playing a trick on you. Check for hidden loudspeakers. Make it clear that you can hear Mum, but because you can't see her, you assume her voice is coming through speakers hidden in the room.

✳ 'But, I'm right here,' Mum will insist. So the other members of the family should turn towards where her voice is coming from, without appearing to see the speaker.

✳ Perhaps one person can walk towards 'invisible' Mum, holding their hands in front of them. When they touch Mum, they can exclaim something like, 'Wow, you really are here. It feels like you. But what have you done to yourself? We can't see you. Can you see us?'

✳ Maybe some people in the room can hold back, frightened to get too close to what seems like a disembodied voice. People close to 'invisible' Mum can reassure them that everything's OK. 'It's all right, Mum is here. Come and feel for yourself.'

✳ Someone could ask 'invisible' Mum to give them her hand, so that she can be led across the room safely. Because she can't be seen, pretend you think that she can't see either and needs a hand to avoid bumping into the furniture.

✳ If 'invisible' Mum leaves the room, keep talking to her as if she is still there.

SILENCE BORES AND SHOW-OFFS

There is a golden rule of which show-offs should be aware. Anyone who is really clever doesn't need to show off. On the other hand, anyone who tries very hard to give the impression of being clever, probably isn't.

The secret of silencing a member of your family whose drivel is driving you bonkers is not to *tell* them to be quiet but to *make* them be quiet, by asking questions they can't answer or replying to things they say with something that sounds very intellectual. Here are some simple but effective lines to use that will silence them once and for all.

SILENCING LINES

* 'I'm interested to hear you say that, because it reminds me that a red blood cell travels round the human body 43,000 times every month.'

* 'You are obviously a genius and remind me of the talented Leonardo da Vinci. After all, Leonardo da Vinci only painted the world's most famous picture, invented breech-loading guns, paddle-wheels, scissors and swimming-belts. He could also write with one hand while he was drawing with his other hand.'

* 'Really? I would have thought that was more a bilateral decentralised transcendence.'

* 'I'm surprised to hear you say that. I always thought that kind of activity was generally regarded as synchronous transfigurative factionalism.'

* 'In that case I wonder how you would respond to the fact that a lead weight and a leaf dropped in a vacuum will fall at exactly the same speed?'

* 'Listening to you, no one would believe that your brain is 80 per cent water.'

* 'That's very interesting. You will also find that the diameter of the earth's orbit is almost exactly 1,000 times the distance that light travels in one second.'

GROW THE LARGEST SUNFLOWER IN THE FAMILY

Sunflowers are some of the easiest plants to grow and they can grow to a spectacular size – over head-height in many cases. So having a family sunflower-growing competition in the summer is easy to organise and simple to judge – the tallest sunflower wins.

GETTING READY FOR GREEN FINGERS

✳ Sunflowers like hot sunshine, so you'll need to prepare a growing area where they will get plenty of sun.

✳ When you buy sunflower seeds, make sure that you select a variety of tall-growing flowers, such as Helianthus 'Russian Giant', which can grow as high as three metres!

✳ There are some varieties of smaller sunflowers that can be grown in containers, but for your family competition, you'll need the tallest sunflowers you can find.

✳ Everyone in the family should be given seeds from the same packet. They should have access to planting tools and water. And – with tall-growing sunflowers – they will need stakes to support them. Once they start to grow, individual sunflowers can get blown around and possibly damaged by wind.

GOING FOR GOLD

1 Each family member should plant one sunflower seed about 5cm deep in the soil. Mark the spot each seed is in with a lolly stick with the name of its family member written on it. Make sure there are about 50cm between each of the seeds to allow them to grow unhindered.

2 Once the seeds are in the ground, it's up to each member of the family to look after their own plant in their own way.

3 They must water their sunflowers.

4 They should find out what kind of fertilizer to feed them and when to apply it.

5 They must also decide when and how to support them as they grow.

6 Measure all the sunflowers regularly to keep track of who is in the lead. The one that grows the tallest is the winner.

HOW TO SURVIVE GOING OVER A WATERFALL

Visiting water parks and enjoying the thrill of being swished down chutes and tubes is great, but being carried over a waterfall isn't fun at all. There's no way of knowing what dangers lie beneath the crashing water and plumes of spray at the bottom.

If the family's dip in a jungle river is suddenly turned into a battle for survival as you are swept towards the edge of a roaring waterfall, this is what you should try to do.

SINK AND SWIM

Just before you go over the waterfall you should jump out and away from the edge. This helps avoid rocks directly at the bottom. Jumping outwards also makes sure that you won't get trapped behind the waterfall.

The safest way of falling down a waterfall is feet first with your arms folded above your head. You should get into this position as you are falling downwards. You'll need to take a deep breath as well, because the water at the bottom may be deep.

On the way down, you should keep your feet squeezed together and your body upright, as if you are standing stiffly to attention, but always keeping your arms above your head.

The moment you hit the water you need to start swimming – even before you rise to the surface. Swimming will help prevent you sinking so far down and it will also get you moving away from the waterfall and into safer water.

Potato Puzzler

There can't be many puzzles that are performed in the kitchen, but here's one to give the family's little grey cells something to grapple with on the vegetable chopping board.

THE SET-UP

1. All you need is a potato and a kitchen knife.

2. Cut a circular slice of potato for each member of the family.

3. Give the knife to everyone in turn and ask them to divide their potato slice into as many pieces as they can – but using just *six* cuts.

4. Pieces can't be readjusted after they have been cut.

5. Nor can they be piled on top of each other after they have been cut.

SWEET SIXTEEN

The diagram below illustrates how a slice of potato can produce 16 pieces in six cuts, but this can be easily beaten. The question is by how many.

See how you all get on. (You'll find the answer on page 191.)

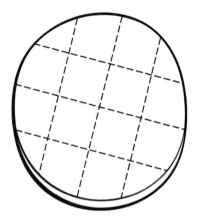

TURN THIS OCTAGON INTO A STAR AND STILL KEEP AN OCTAGON

Look carefully at this shape. There's an octagon inside another octagon – nothing complicated there. Ask the other members of the family to study the shape as well. Then announce that they've got to come up with a way of cutting the shape into eight pieces, all the same size and shape, and all created in such a way that they can be put together again to form an eight-pointed star, which also has an octagon in the middle.

Go on, admit it. That is a bit more complicated. (You'll find the answer to this on page 191.)

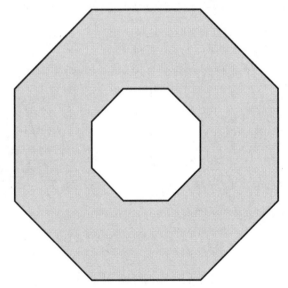

THE SET-UP

1 Ask everyone to make an exact copy of this shape.

2 Give them scissors, rulers and pencils.

3 Set the clock and see who is the quickest to figure out the solution.

Convince Your Family That You Are A Mind-Reader

There are two parts to this amazing feat of mental agility. The first part is clever, because you appear to use mind-reading powers to work out a number inside someone's head. The second is an absolute brainstormer, because you reveal a number that somebody has left out of a calculation completely at random! How could you possibly know what that was?

THINK OF A NUMBER

1 Ask someone in the family to think of a number.

2 Ask them to double it.

3 Ask them to add 5.

4 Now, add 12.

5 Subtract 3.

6 Divide in half.

7 Subtract the number they first thought of.

8 Now announce that the number they have arrived at is 7.

9 Never let on that the answer is *always* 7 – even though it works out at 7 every time!

LUCKY NUMBER 7

See how it works in practice:

1 Think of a number	say 37	
2 Double it	74	
3 Add 5	79	
4 Add 12	91	

5 Subtract 3   88

6 Divide in half   44

7 Subtract the number first thought of   – 37

8 And the answer is   7

THINK OF A DIFFERENT NUMBER

1 Ask someone else in the family to think of a different number.

2 Ask them to multiply it by 100.

3 Ask them to add 36.

4 Now get them to subtract the number they first thought of.

5 Ask them to tell you the digits in their total *except for one digit*, which they keep to themselves.

6 You then add the digits you do know together, subtract their sum from the next highest multiple of 9 and the answer will give you the missing digit.

HIDE AND SEEK

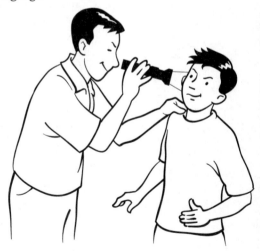

Here's an example to show how it works:

1 Think of a number   say 94

2 Multiply it by 100   9400

3 Add 36   9436

4 Subtract the first number   – 94
                                        9342

5 Ask to be told the digits except for one   342

6 Add 3 + 4 + 2   9

7 Subtract 9 from 18 (the next highest multiple of 9) and the missing digit is: 9

Now let anyone try to say that you aren't a mind-reader!

SEND MESSAGES WITH SEMAPHORE

How cool would it be to have a family signal system? For example, when Dad's gone down to the beach to get ice creams all round you could signal a change of order to him instead of shouting.

SAY HELLO TO SEMAPHORE

Semaphore is a signalling system that spells out letters (and numbers) by holding a pair of flags in particular positions.

You hold the flags, with your arms straight, in the positions shown below, so that the person you are signalling to can read words such as HUGE, CHOCOLATE and ICE CREAM letter by letter.

Some of the flag positions represent numbers as well as letters, and some have special meanings, for example to show numbers will follow, or that the person sending the signal has made a mistake and wants to correct it.

Semaphore is something everyone in the family can learn, by practising alone in front of the mirror and then together in the garden.

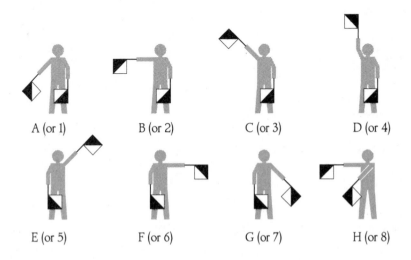

A (or 1) B (or 2) C (or 3) D (or 4)

E (or 5) F (or 6) G (or 7) H (or 8)

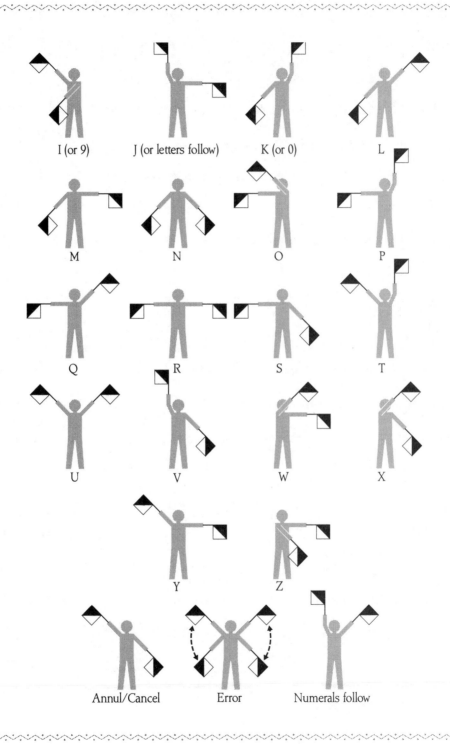

I (or 9)   J (or letters follow)   K (or 0)   L

M   N   O   P

Q   R   S   T

U   V   W   X

Y   Z

Annul/Cancel   Error   Numerals follow

How To Find Water In The Desert

There's no need for your family to panic if the holiday car breaks down and you are stuck in the desert for the night. The desert may appear to be dry and dusty, but there is water to be found if you know where to look for it.

DIGGING FOR WATER

There is a lot more water below the desert surface than most people realise. As soon as the sun sets and the air becomes cooler, the family can start digging in likely places. The question is what should the family be looking for?

* A likely spot is often at the base of the steep side of a sand dune or a rocky outcrop.

* Small bushes or patches of scrub may indicate water below the surface round their roots, so someone could try digging there.

* If there are animal trails, they could lead to a place where animals drink. Somebody could explore the trails for a short distance to see if there are signs of water.

* The ground itself can produce water, even in the desert. This needs to be collected at night and the way to do this is to start by digging a hole slightly less than a metre across.

* Place an open container in the bottom of the hole to catch the drips.

* Spread a sheet of plastic over the hole, fixing it with stones at the edge. Then place a stone in the middle to weight it down.

✳ Water vapour in the ground will collect on the underside of the plastic and run down into the container beneath.

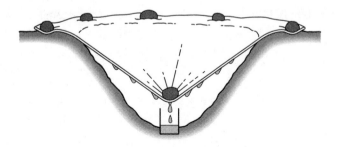

COLLECTING DEW

It can get cold in the desert at night and dew often forms. Your family can collect this from the metal panels and windows of the car and keep it to drink.

✳ The dew should be carefully soaked up in cloths and wrung out over a collecting dish.

✳ Places where dew might run down, like door windows, should have cloths wedged at the bottom to collect moisture that forms during the night.

✳ Dew also collects on stones and smooth pebbles. So members of the family can collect lots of these and put them on a suitable surface like a sheet of plastic, a rubber ground sheet or the inside of a curved metal panel removed from the car: the bonnet maybe.

SAFE DRINKING

Even water collected in this way should be treated to remove things that could make you ill *before* you drink it. Your family medical kit may well have special tablets to purify water. If it doesn't, you could light a fire and boil the water to make it safe to drink (there are instructions on how to light a fire on page 100). Getting stuck in the desert on holiday is bad enough, but you don't want to follow that by being stuck in bed with an upset tummy!

Vanquish Vampires

So Dad innocently booked a holiday in Transylvania and the family arrives to find the hotel is right next door to a dodgy-looking castle. Worse still, there's talk amongst the guests about things going bump in the night. It's time to face facts – the hotel is haunted.

One of the scariest things about a vampire attack is that victims don't remember anything about what happened to them. Vampires have a way of hypnotising their victims, which means that they can return to attack them time after time until all a victim's blood has been sucked away. So if Mum wakes up looking pale and sickly and can't remember anything about the evening before, don't assume she just had too much wine with her meal. Sometimes the only evidence of a vampire attack is two little pinpricks in the neck, where a vampire's fangs have punctured the skin to suck out the fresh human blood they need to stay 'alive'. Casually check Mum's neck for telltale signs.

KEEPING VAMPIRES AT BAY

Vampires can turn their victims into vampires themselves. So when it comes to protecting the family you can't take too many precautions! Vampires are driven away by garlic, so make sure the family chomps on plenty of garlic at every meal. Ask the hotel chef for cloves of garlic and hang them by the doors and windows in your rooms. Vampires are scared away by fire, so make sure you always have candles on your table in the restaurant, and that Dad always carries a box of matches.

VAMPIRE SLAYERS

When you finally admit that those people you thought were just batty guests are really the undead, and that the hotel is overrun with vampires, it's time to act. The most common method of ending a vampire's reign of terror is to drive a wooden stake through its heart. Alternatively use a large, red-hot nail. Boiling a vampire's heart in oil is said to be a sure way of stopping it returning from the grave ever again. The same goes for cutting off a vampire's head with a gravedigger's spade. Good luck.

KITE KIT

Sled kites are easy to make and fly. Before you begin to make one you'll need to collect:

✳ 2 sheets of A3 copier paper (297mm x 420mm)

✳ 2 wooden barbecue skewers 300mm long

✳ A long ruler, or other straight-edged piece of wood

✳ A pencil

✳ Strong sticky tape

✳ A reel of sewing thread

✳ Scissors

ASSEMBLY INSTRUCTIONS

1 Fold one sheet of A3 paper in half and then fold it in half again in the same direction. Then open the sheet flat again.

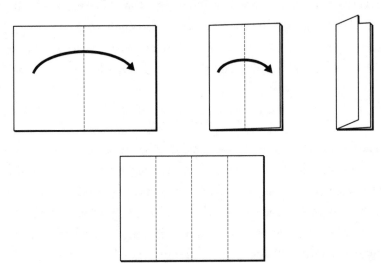

2 Measure down 105mm from each of the top corners and mark with a pencil. Now draw a line from the mark to the top of the outer fold and then to the bottom of the same fold. Repeat on the other side. Cut off the four corner triangles. Fold and crease both side wings into the centre and then open out flat again.

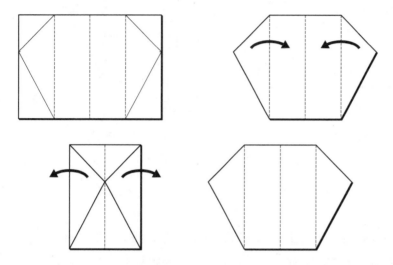

3 Lay the skewers in the folds and stick them into place with short strips of sticky tape. Fold the sticky tape around the wing tips as shown below, then make a small hole in each tip with a scissor point.

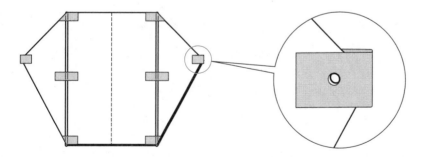

④ Cut three 50mm wide strips of paper from the other sheet of paper and stick them together with tape to make one long tail. Then stick each end of the tail to the bottom of the skewers to make a loop.

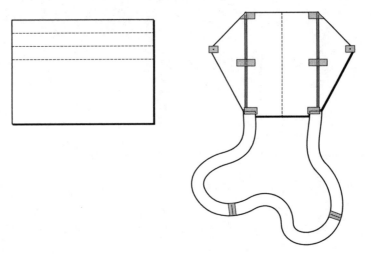

⑤ Cut a one-metre length of thread and tie each end through the holes in the wing tips. Tie an overhand knot exactly in the centre of the thread to make a towing point. Tie the end of the reel of thread to the towing point – and you're now ready to fly!

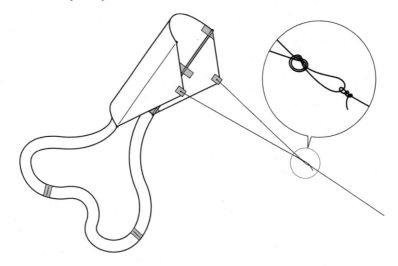

GOING CRACKERS

Who's the biggest eater in the family? Who guzzles more chips than anyone else? Who's the crisp chomping champion? Who always wants second helpings of everything? Who can eat a whole packet of biscuits in a sitting?

Whoever it is, how difficult do you think they would find eating three cream crackers in a minute? It's time to make every member of the family take the challenge.

SUPERHUMAN TASK

Three cream crackers doesn't seem like an enormous amount of food to consume in sixty seconds, but try it and learn something – it's a superhuman task!

It's not the amount of food that's the problem, it's the texture. Cream crackers are extremely dry and you'll find that you can't produce enough saliva to eat and swallow three in a minute; that's an average of one every twenty seconds. You're not allowed to have a glass of water on hand while you attempt this challenge.

Anyone who has a go will almost certainly end up with a mouthful of crumbs (most of which will be stuck to the roof of their mouth) and a desperate need for a large drink of water.

CREATE A FAMILY SCRAPBOOK

Photographs bring back memories of fun things your family has done together. But what about the other things that formed a part of all those activities – holidays, days out, celebrations, birthdays? They are memory milestones as well, but how often are they kept? If you gather them into a scrapbook, you can include all kinds of bits and pieces that capture memories of their own – just like a family photo album, but with much more variety.

Mum may not want to be reminded of that horrible dress she wore when it was the height of fashion. Dad might be embarrassed about the time he tried to order lunch in a foreign language and the waiter brought completely different food. But keep the magazine page that gave Mum the idea for the outfit, and the bill from Dad's holiday restaurant and you can paste these into the family scrapbook as a permanent reminder. So the next time Mum asks, 'You're not going out dressed like

that, are you?' or Dad gets grumpy about a
school French test that didn't go too well, you
just reach for the scrapbook, turn to the right
page and point at it with a knowing smile before
mentioning something about the 'pot calling
the kettle black'.

ALL IN THE FAMILY

Get into the habit of checking if something is
worth keeping for the scrapbook before you get
rid of it. Every family has things which may not
seem to be very interesting at the time, but
which later on can trigger all sorts of memories.

Airline tickets, luggage labels, hotel and
restaurant bills, postcards, shop paper bags, hand-written
directions or maps from local people will add dozens of memories to
the photographs taken on the same holidays. (Look at the list of suggestions for
Holiday Scavengers on page 43 to get some inspiration.)

Closer to home, you can paste in cinema tickets from the time you saw a great
family film, or the entry tickets to somewhere special visited on a family day out.
Leaflets about places you've visited with your school, welcome notes from new
teachers, cards awarded for good work – put all these in the scrapbook and remind
Mum and Dad about them when they get all serious about a school report that
seems to be describing someone rather different!

Use the family scrapbook to record memorable Christmases, too. The terrible
jokes inside the crackers, the paper hat Dad was wearing when the unfortunate
photograph pasted next to it was taken, the home-made gift cards, the carefully
coloured-in Christmas card shaped like a Christmas tree which you made for Mum
in your first term at school – all of these are special in their own way, and all of them
can easily be saved in a family scrapbook for people to laugh at and cringe over for
years to come.

How To Find North And South By Reading The Stars

Getting lost is scary, and after dark it's scarier still. At midnight – when the family is lost, cold, tired and worried that they won't be able to find their way until morning light – it's time to step up and be a hero.

And the hero will be the person who remembers reading this page of this book.

FOLLOWING THE PLOUGH

As long as you can see the stars, you can lead the family to safety. In the northern hemisphere you can find the North Star, Polaris, quite easily. Search the sky for the group of seven stars known as the Plough or the Big Dipper. Find the two 'pointer' stars at one end. Follow a line between these stars and you'll come to Polaris. Once you've found that, you know where north is. Now mark the line with two stones and in the morning you can get your bearings right and find your way to safety.

THE SOUTHERN CROSS

Cross may be the way the Southern family feel when they realise they are lost, but be thankful the Southern Cross in the night sky is a star signpost in the southern hemisphere. This isn't as easy to find or use as the Plough in the northern hemisphere, but if the family is lost in the Australian outback, or a jungle in South-east Asia, they'll be grateful for it all the same.

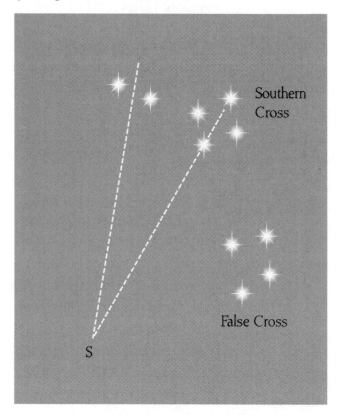

The Southern Cross is made up of four bright stars in the shape of a cross. Don't be misled by the False Cross, which has dimmer stars set farther apart. Take a line through the cross and a line down between the two bright stars to its left. The point where those lines cross is south. Now mark the line with two stones and in the morning you can get your bearings right and find your way to safety.

How To Play Achi On The Beach

Sand makes a perfect surface to mark out the board for this popular West African game. It's easy to set up and great for providing some gentle entertainment after a tiring day of sunbathing and relaxing.

THE BOARD

You can make a big Achi board, if you want to, using rocks as counters. Alternatively mark out a smaller one using pebbles. The choice is yours, but the game is played in the same way in either case.

THE GAME

1. Two players have four counters each.

2. Taking it in turn, they place their counters on the board on empty points, wherever the lines intersect.

3. Once all eight counters are in place each player in turn moves one of their counters along a line to an empty point.

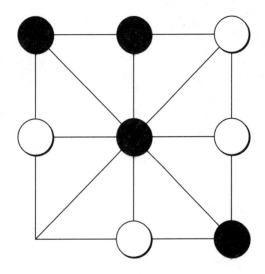

4. The object of the game is to get three counters in a row; the first player to do this is the winner.

5. In this example, black is the first to get three counters in a row.

TIE A KNOT WITHOUT LETTING GO OF EITHER END

This is a seriously knotty problem that will have even the family brainbox getting into a big twist trying to work it out.

PREPARATION IS THE SECRET

The secret of tying a knot in a piece of string without letting go of either end is to start in the right way.

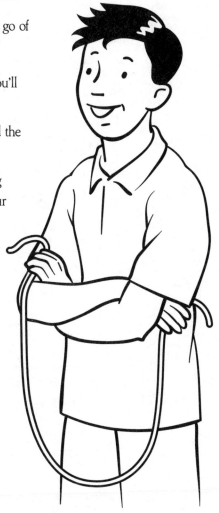

1. Don't just grab hold of the string at random, because you'll get nowhere.

2. Instead, fold your arms across your chest, having placed the piece of string within easy reach.

3. Keeping your arms folded, pick up one end of the string in your right hand and the other end of the string in your left hand.

4. Then slowly unfold your arms, without letting go of the string.

5. When your arms are unfolded, there'll be a knot in the string!

What's happened, of course, is that the 'knot' in your arms has been transferred to the knot in the string.

Do-It-Yourself Printing Press

You can't get to a photocopier. The household's scanner is being repaired. You can't cut what you want to copy out of the newspaper because someone else wants to read it. What do you do?

The answer is simple – make your own copy on your own printing press!

PRINTING MATERIALS

Search round the house and collect the following:

* A cup of water
* Half a cup of turpentine
* A dollop of washing-up liquid
* A glass jar
* A paint brush
* A sheet of plastic
* A few sheets of clean white A4 paper

* A piece of wood large enough to cover an A4 sheet of paper

* A weight to press the wood down

WET OFF THE PRESS

1 Mix the water, turpentine and washing-up liquid in the jar to make the printing 'ink'.

2 Lay the plastic sheet on a flat surface and place the newspaper article you want to copy on top of it facing up.

3 Use the brush to carefully paint the surface of the article with the 'ink' from the jar.

4 Lay a sheet of A4 paper over the 'inked' article.

5 Carefully place the wood over the paper and press down on it (using the weight if need be), taking care not to move the paper beneath because the copy will smudge.

6 Peel back the white paper and you will see that the underside has a copy of the article it was pressed against.

7 This is a reverse copy, however. You can hold it in front of a mirror, which will make it possible to read, if you want to. But making a copy the right way round is more satisfactory.

8 To do this, you must wait until your reverse copy is dry. Then you repeat the printing process, but this time you make your copy from the reverse printing you have already made.

9 When your second pressing is completed (with a new piece of white paper, of course), it will be a mirror image of a mirror image. In other words, it will be a copy of the original newspaper article, only it will be the right way round.

10 Now all you need to do is make sure that the newspaper dries out thoroughly for whoever wants to read it after you, while your own copy is drying as well.

Escape From A Car Perched Over A Cliff

Now is not the time to start blaming anyone for what's happened. The fate of the family is in the balance – literally. One false move and things could get a lot, lot worse.

WEIGHING UP THE SITUATION

You may not have much time, so every move you make has to be the right one. How is the car balanced? Is the heaviest part hanging over the cliff? Or is it the lightest part? Most cars have their greatest weight in the front where the engine is

found. If the back of the car is not over the edge, you probably have more time to climb out.

How secure is the car? Does it move when you shift your weight even a little? If the car slips, time isn't on your side!

BE POSITIVE, BUT STEADY

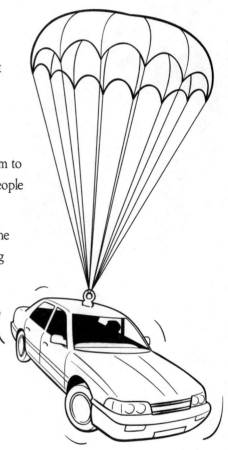

1 Check whether the front doors are over land. If they are, use them to escape from the car, whichever way it is facing. Make sure the people in the back of the car climb forward and escape first.

2 If the front doors are over the cliff edge, you'll have to move to the back of the car. Before you leave the front seats, pick up anything sharp or heavy that may be to hand: you may need this to get out. If a possible 'escape tool' is in the back, don't pick this up until you are in the back.

3 Don't jump into the back. Move slowly and positively. If there are two or more people moving from front to back, they should move together, not one at a time.

4 If you can open the back doors without making the car slide over the cliff, open them slowly and get out fast.

5 If the car has no back doors, or if it is too dangerous to open them, you'll have to break a window to escape. Not the back window, though – climbing out through that would cause too much movement. One of the windows in the side of the car is better.

6 Use your 'escape tool' to smash the centre of the window; cars have windows made from safety glass, so you won't be hurt.

7 Push out the broken glass and then slide through the window to safety.

8 Once you're safe move away from the edge of the cliff, in case the car topples over and a piece of the cliff top breaks away with it.

CREATE A FAMILY PERCUSSION SECTION

The percussion section of an orchestra is where the drums, cymbals and all the other instruments that are struck to produce sounds are grouped together. There are many different kinds of percussion instruments: triangles, bells, glockenspiels – and then there are those which you can make and play at home.

STRIKE UP THE MUSIC

With a little imagination you can create percussion instruments for everyone in the family – some might even need two people to play them. Remember hitting anything made of glass *really* hard is never a good idea. If it smashes, the concert might end sooner than expected. In fact, it's probably a good idea to use wooden spoons or wooden forks to strike the 'instruments' – not metal ones.

∗ Saucepan drums – turn saucepans upside down and bang their bases.

∗ Glass bells – line up 12 glasses side by side, with a gap two fingers wide between them. Pour water into each glass in increasing amounts, so that the glass at one end has the lowest level of water and the glass at the opposite end has the highest level of water. Strike them gently and each glass will produce a different note.

∗ Bucket bongos – sit down holding an upturned bucket between your knees and bang the base with your fingers and hands. If you have buckets of different sizes, stand these in a row upside down and they'll each produce a different tone when struck.

∗ Rhythm sticks – two pieces of round wood 30cm long and about as thick as a broom handle can be knocked together to set up a steady beat.

DUCK FOR APPLES

This is a traditional game that people have enjoyed for hundreds of years. It's popular at Hallowe'en, when it's played indoors, but it's also great fun in the garden on hot summer days. You play the game the same way wherever you are – the only difference is that you should put down a big waterproof sheet to play on if you are going to duck for apples inside the house.

YOU WILL NEED

* A large tub, or other waterproof container, at least 35cm deep

* Enough clean water to fill the tub or container to a depth of at least 30cm

* At least twice as many apples as there are people playing (leave the stalks on some and remove the stalks from the rest)

AIM OF THE GAME

This is easy. When you duck for apples you try to lift an apple from the water using just your mouth – no hands, arms, feet, other parts of your body, or any equipment are allowed – only your mouth.

1 Pour in the water and add the apples.

2 Take turns to try to catch a stalk between your teeth to avoid getting wet.

3 Or ... you can open your mouth wide, aim your teeth at an apple and plunge your head into the water, driving the apple to the bottom, where you can bite into it. Then flip yourself upright – you'll be soaking wet but the winner (hopefully).

4 The fastest to catch an apple wins.

HOW TO BE THE GHOULIEST FAMILY IN THE NEIGHBOURHOOD

When Hallowe'en comes around and you're determined to convince the neighbours that they're living next to the real-life Addams Family, you've got to look the part. Don't listen to people who insist that the only way to be seriously ghoulish is to be spotted climbing out of holes in the ground at night. Appearance is everything.

Since children generally look like their parents, here are two ghoulish characters you can adapt for your own use. Dad is one. Mum is the other and the kids can choose to be one or the other – or maybe a really scary combination of both.

SCARY SKELETON

1 Concentrate on the skull; the rest of the skeleton can be hidden beneath a billowing sheet.

2 Make your face ghostly white using face cream and powder.

3 Paint large black circles around your eyes with eyeliner.

4 Use eyeliner to paint your nose black, so that it looks like a hollow in the front of the skull.

5 You need eyeliner to make your cheeks look hollow as well. Trace the outline of the bones in your face and then fill in the areas inside with eyeliner.

6 Use eyeliner to paint a row of teeth above your mouth and

another below it, so it looks like two ghastly, ghostly, jaws opening when you open your mouth. Painting a couple of these teeth black will make you look even more frightening.

7 Draw the lines of skull cracks along your forehead and under your eyes. The ones under your eyes can join up with the black cheeks.

8 Welcome Scary Skeleton.

MONSTER WITH THE MELTING FACE

1 You'll need: glue that is safe when used on your skin, cotton-wool balls, dried peas or beans, food colouring, flour, water, and syrup.

2 Begin by sticking clumps of cotton-wool over your face. Aim to create an uneven surface with bulges and lumps in a few places.

3 Make a thick paste using the dried peas or beans, some flour, two tablespoons of syrup and water. Add the food colouring of choice to make the 'skin' look suitably ghoulish.

4 Spread the paste over your face, beginning with your forehead and then moving down to your chin.

5 You can use a hair-dryer to dry the mix, *but* don't hold it too close to your face to avoid burning yourself.

6 Dress in clothes that are too big for you – so that they flap and hang loose on your body – and your whole body will look as if it's melting away.

THE HOLLY AND THE IVY AND EVERYTHING ELSE IN A GREEN CHRISTMAS

Christmas is the season of good will – at least that's what it's meant to be. Unfortunately a lot of what a family does at Christmas can be very harmful to the planet, not to mention harmful to their bank accounts.

But it doesn't have to be like this. Christmas can be just as enjoyable and maybe even more memorable if you decide to have a green Christmas. This can save trees. It can reduce waste. A green Christmas uses less energy – and, it can save everyone in the family a lot of money.

SEASON'S GREETINGS

✳ E-cards are a good way to save money as well as the planet at Christmas. Instead of buying and posting lots of cards, use a computer to design cards of your own. They'll be more personal than shop-bought cards. You can add messages to the people you're sending them to, and you can e-mail them to everyone – saving paper envelopes, money for stamps and fuel to deliver them.

DECK THE HALLS

* Before plastic decorations and silver tinsel, Christmas decorations were entirely green. Provided you aren't greedy and use too much, there's no reason why your family Christmas can't be decorated in the traditional way as well. Holly (without berries – birds need to feed on them in winter), ivy, and a few evergreen branches can transform your home.

If you go out collecting these decorations as a family, be careful that you don't damage the trees you take them from. Be very careful as well about picking mistletoe because some varieties are becoming very scarce and should be allowed to grow, not picked so that Mum and Dad can kiss each other underneath it.

* The biggest decoration is the Christmas tree. Each year millions are dug up to be used for a few weeks and then thrown away. What a waste of trees. What a waste of money! Why not buy a tree with roots that is in a pot. After Christmas put it outside and keep the roots fed and watered. It will grow happily in the garden until you bring it inside next Christmas.

D-I-Y DECORATIONS

* You don't need shiny plastic balls and flashy lines of stars to add colour to Christmas. Tree decorations can be made from dough, which is baked and painted. Popcorn and peanuts (in their shells) can be threaded together to make strings of decorations. Oranges and tangerines decorated with cloves make attractive features and decorated cardboard packaging can be recycled to make exciting decorations you won't find in any shops. With recycling in mind, all of these decorations can be composted when Christmas is over, so nothing is wasted.

SEASON OF GIVING

Christmas presents don't need to be expensive to be memorable and meaningful. You can show the rest of the family how much they mean to you in plenty of ways that don't involve battling through crowds of Christmas shoppers to spend your hard-earned money on things they may never use.

✳ Instead of giving 'things', why not give special treats – a trip to a film, or the theatre; a visit to an exhibition; a day out somewhere special?

✳ You could offer to do something for someone that they would really appreciate – keeping the garden tidy; washing a car; cleaning windows.

✳ Maybe you could use your creative skills to make presents from recycled things at home? Cardboard tubes, individually decorated, can make lovely napkin rings. Empty cereal boxes, glued together and decorated attractively can be great for filing papers. Empty jam jars, decorated with enamel paints, make ideal garden illuminations when tea lights are lit inside them.

✳ Perhaps there's a present the whole family could use – a new radio or a long-lasting torch? You can even get green versions of appliances like these which wind up and don't use mains electricity or throwaway batteries.

✳ Then there are green presents that spread good will far beyond your family. You can sponsor a rainforest, adopt an endangered animal, plant a tree and give people other kinds of long-lasting gifts that will make a difference to the whole planet long after other things you might have given have been forgotten about.

MAKE A FAMILY ROGUES' GALLERY

Here's a classic way to create a picture gallery of real and imagined family members. Each person needs a sheet of paper and a pencil.

1. First everyone draws a face on a piece of paper. Then they fold it, so that the face is hidden, and pass the paper to the person on their right.

2. Now everyone draws a body and a pair of arms on the piece of paper they have received. Again, the paper is folded to hide what has just been drawn and passed to the right.

3. The next parts of the 'rogue' to be added are the legs. When these have been drawn, the papers are passed to the right once more for the feet. Again, the paper is folded to hide what has just been drawn and passed to the right.

4. Finally, everyone writes the name of a real or imaginary family member on the bottom of the page. It could be Great Aunt Enid from Patagonia or Dad.

5. When all the drawings have been completed all the strips are gathered in and unfolded one by one, so that everyone can admire the masterpieces they have created together and have a good laugh at them!

ANSWERS TO THE PUZZLES

Here's the place to check all your answers – put yourself out of your misery
before the puzzles drive you mad and the family ends up arguing!

TRYING TRIANGLES (page 21)

There are 35 triangles in the diagram.

BOGGLE YOUR BRAIN WITH 'ABRACADABRA' (page 33)

There are 1,024 ways to spell ABRACADABRA

DUMBFOUND THE FAMILY WITH DOODLES (page 36)

1. A giraffe passing a second-storey window
2. A spider performing the splits
3. A dachshund passing a gap in a fence
4. A koala bear climbing the far side of a eucalyptus tree
5. A black snake on a zebra crossing
6. A microbe affected by penicillin being avoided by its neighbours
7. A mouse hiding behind a stone
8. A spider performing a handstand

SOLVE ROMAN NUMBER PUZZLES (page 46)

1. IV + I = V
2. VII — V = II
3. II — I = I
4. Look at the puzzle upside down!

SPY CATCHER (page 47)

Start with the letter with the dot (S.). Counting S as one, count every thirteenth letter in a clockwise direction to decode the message:

CONVOY LEAVES THURSDAY

HEARTBREAK HOTEL (page 68)

Beware – the way the question is phrased is intended to mislead you.
The £2 which the bellboy took should not be added to the £27 the men paid.
It should be subtracted, because the £2 the bellboy got is part of the £27
the three men paid altogether. If you subtract the £2 from the £27 you get
the £25 that is in the hotel's till.

QUARTER A CIRCLE WITH THREE EQUAL LINES (page 83)

Divide the diameter of the circle into four equal parts. Then draw semicircles on each side of the diameter, as shown. There's your solution.

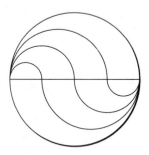

PUZZLE THE FAMILY WITH RIDDLES (page 94)

1 An apple
2 A map
3 The moon

4 Her baby before it is born

5 An echo

6 The man was bald

7 The boy's grandfather in the riddle is his mother's father, not his father's father

8 A secret

9 A watermelon

10 A clock

SQUARE CUTS (page 112)

Challenge 1

The square needs to be divided by two straight cuts like this to form a perfect square:

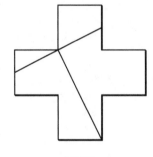
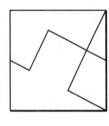

Challenge 2

The diagram needs to be divided into four pieces like this to form a perfect square:

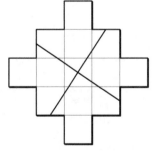
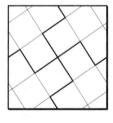

CONNECT THESE NINE DOTS WITH FOUR LINES (page 126)

The four lines should be drawn like this:

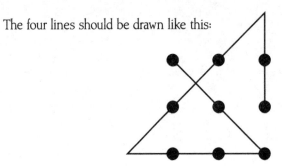

HOW TO MAKE THIS UNEVEN
CARPET SQUARE WITH JUST THREE CUTS (page 142)

Make the three cuts like this:

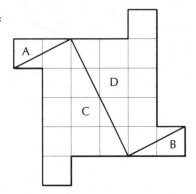

Assemble the pieces to make a square carpet like this:

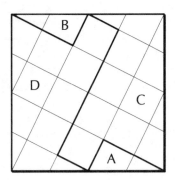

POTATO PUZZLER (page 154)

As many as 22 pieces of potato may be obtained by using the six cuts. The illustration shows a fairly symmetrical solution.

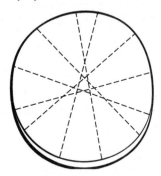

The rule in such cases is that every cut shall intersect every other cut and that no two intersections shall coincide. That is to say that every line must pass through every other line, but no more than two lines should intersect anywhere. There are other ways of making the cuts, but this rule must always be observed if you are going to get the full number of pieces.

TURN THIS OCTAGON INTO A STAR
AND STILL KEEP AN OCTAGON (page 155)

This is how the octagon can be formed into a star as required:

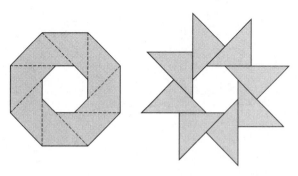

Also available in this bestselling series:

The Boys' Book: How To Be The Best At Everything
ISBN: 978-1-905158-64-5
Price: £7.99

The Girls' Book: How To Be The Best At Everything
(number one children's bestseller)
ISBN: 978-1-905158-79-9
Price: £7.99

The Mums' Book: For The Mum Who's Best At Everything
(*The Sunday Times* number one bestseller)
ISBN: 978-1-84317-246-8
Price: £9.99

The Dads' Book: For The Dad Who's Best At Everything
ISBN: 978-1-84317-250-5
Price: £9.99

And coming soon for Christmas 2007:

The Christmas Book: How To Have The Best Christmas Ever
ISBN: 978-1-84317-282-6
Price: £9.99

These titles and all other Michael O'Mara titles are available by post from:
Bookpost Ltd.,
PO Box 29,
Douglas,
Isle of Man,
IM99 1BQ

Credit cards are accepted, please:
Telephone: 01624 677237
Fax: 01624 670923
Email: bookshop@enterprise.net
Internet: www.bookpost.co.uk

Postage and packing is free in the UK,
overseas customers should allow £5 per hardback book.